THOUGHT CATALOG BOOKS

Read This If

Read This If

A Collection of Essays that Prove Someone Else Gets it, Too

THOUGHT CATALOG

Thought Catalog Books

Brooklyn, NY

THOUGHT CATALOG BOOKS

Copyright © 2016 by The Thought & Expression Co.

First edition, 2016

ISBN 978-1533014665

10 9 8 7 6 5 4 3 2 1

Cover photography by © pixabay.com

Contents

1

Read This If Nobody Texted You Good Morning

Heidi Priebe

First of all: Good morning, beautiful.

Is it too late to say that? I know you've probably been awake a while — likely hours or even all day. I know you may have gone this whole time without hearing it — shrugging back to friends and family who asked you how you're doing with a non-committal "Fine" because that is what we're meant to do as humans – answer meaningful questions with arbitrary phrases. I know that you may not be fine. I know you may have had a lacklustre day. And I know that something as incredibly mundane as a "Good morning" text may have made all the difference in the world. It's okay if that's the case. It's okay to sometimes ache for those simple and kind-hearted gestures.

Because the truth is that good morning texts are more than a half-hearted means of communication. They are a sign that we are thought of. Cared for. Adored, by someone who may not be immediately present. They are a reminder — one we perhaps should not need but sometimes do — that we are appreciated in our entireties. So if you did not get one this morning, here is what I want you to know:

You deserve to have a good day today. Not because of some universal law that necessitates good things happening to worthwhile people, but because we all do. We all deserve to have a beautiful morning and a correspondingly fantastic day, regardless of who loves us or appreciates us or thinks of us first thing when they wake up in the AM. Just because someone is not around to appreciate the complexities of who you are does not mean that you deserve anything less than pure joy. And in case there's no one else to remind you, here is what else I want you to know:

There's a particular way you laugh that can make an entire room light up, if only for a moment in time. There is a way you tilt your head when you are concentrating that makes you look unbearably kissable — as if you were placed on this earth only to stare at things and frown in the most endearing form humanely possible. There is a noise you make when you are falling asleep — a soft, almost inaudible sigh that sounds like the ethereal embodiment of all that is tranquil and calm. There are a thousand minute intricacies that make up the tapestry of who you are and not a single one has ceased to exist since the last time that somebody loved you.

I know we're not supposed to need reminders of that. I know that we're supposed to be strong and self-sufficient and reassured — certain of our own worth, questioning only the value of others. But we're human. We forget.

We forget that we are lovable. We forget that we're desired. We forget that we are anything other than the hard-shelled, busybody workaholics that we've all been trained to behave as. We forget that we, too, merit adoration.

And here's what it's easiest to forget: Who you are doesn't cease to exist because there's nobody there to admire it. The way you bite your pencil is still cute, even when there's nobody to tease you for it. The way you hold yourself still exudes confidence, even if there's no one to assert it to. The way your eyes light up when you're talking about what you love is — and endlessly will be — attractive, regardless of who is there to listen to you speak. All the little quirks that make you up are not extinguished because somebody once chose against them. You still deserve to have a good day, even when there's no one there to wish it to you. Even if you forget to remind yourself.

Someday someone's going to love all of those tiny things about you. Someone's going to love the way you cough. They're going to laugh at the way you lose your keys while you're actually holding them. Someday, someone is going to stare at you from across a crowded room and know exactly how you're feeling based on the way your head is tilting or the type of wine you've used to fill your glass. Someone is going to appreciate all of your obscurities eventually but right now they are all only your own. And that's okay. First and foremost, you will always belong to yourself.

Here's what I urge of you if you did not receive a good morning text today: Don't forget about what makes you incredible. Don't let your own intricacies slide. Because the lovable parts of you are not gone — I absolutely promise you that much.

You are so much more than the person who nobody texted this morning. You are encompassing. You are fierce. You are a blazing, roaring fire in a world full of people who've been burnt. So please, refuse to let the wounded people extinguish you. Refuse to be tamed. Refuse to flicker down into a meagre, burnt-out coal because somebody else is not tending to your flame.

At the end of the day, we're all in charge of what we bring to our lives. So be the person who brings light to your own, even if nobody else shows up to it. Be the person who has a good day, even if nobody wishes it to them. Find a way to fuel your flame when no one else remembers to, because the world needs the light you give off.

And you, my dear, are too intense a power to be reduced by something as small and insignificant as the lack of a good morning text.

2

Read This If It Feels Like Your Depression Is Getting The Best Of You

Kendra Syrdal

Around you the sun keeps rising and setting. The traffic keeps pressing through in the most unrelenting way. The clouds rolls by, the holidays happen. Everyone talks about how they can't believe October is over and winter is almost here. And you smile behind steaming cider as if you're just excited as them.

But really, if you were being truly honest, you'd admit that nothing has felt different since August. Rather everything feels blurry, muffled. You've lost track of the days and the nights because instead of being individual sunrises and sunsets, it's just another day of you feeling like you're walking upstream against a raging current. And instead of fighting, instead of it feeling like a challenge, you're just getting tired.

Too many times you've just lain in bed avoiding any and every responsibility. You don't know when the last time you checked your mail was. It's probably overflowing with unanswered letters from cable companies (thank god for automatic withdrawal) and catalogs filled with girls who had enough energy to wash their hair that morning. You sit in the tub watching the now lukewarm water draining beneath you and you wish for a second that you'd go down with it into some abyss where there are not problems outside of wondering where the end of the pipe will take you.

The stereotypical depressed person is always in the dark maybe with ugly, forlorn, black, mascara streaks painting her cheeks or maybe with staring with his bloodshot, red eyes from popping vessels while sobbing. And they sit alone, still in the dark, with that unnecessary war paint, contemplating how much better the world would be without them. And even though that's a stereotype, sometimes that monster comes in rearing it's nasty head and messes everything up.

As terrible as the extreme depression, the scary feeling of doom that exists, more often than not, it's a different monster. And it's a monster that doesn't exist in the crazy highs or lows and because of that; it isn't as easy to spot. It hangs out in the corners undetected just waiting until it can latch on and never let go.

Depression sometimes is a feeling of utter desolation, but what about when it isn't?

Sarah Silverman recently described depression as the feeling of homesickness, but you're home so there's no way to satiate the feeling. I couldn't agree or relate more. It's knowing you have no real reason to not be ecstatic, to not be happy, but instead of feeling anything all you can feel is unenthused, sulky, static.

It's seeing all of the crayons laid out in front of you, the entire 120-count Crayola box you always coveted in grade school, every single color you could possibly imagine. It's seeing them and having the ability to pick any color, but only being able to force yourself back to the same broken grey crayon day after day after day.

It's watching people promote asinine things like "drinking more tea" and "running for the endorphins" and thinking, "Fine. I'll give it a fucking shot." But then your bladder is bursting from your 18th cup of stupid chamomile and your shins are aching from running for hours, but even after heeding all of this naturopathic bullshit you still just want to sit on the kitchen floor and eventually blend into your surroundings, ceasing to be you because being you is getting exhausting.

It's hearing about how Prozac changed someone's life and how therapy is their everything, so you keep popping open the little orange bottle and talking about your ex-best friend and your fears every Thursday. You do all of the things you're supposed to do but nothing's different. It's researching at 4 AM for any possible answer but still not wanting to smile at jokes on Twitter or text anyone back because you just suck. And if you know it they must know it too.

It's feeling like the same bland, sad, murky version of yourself day after day and just wondering if this is how the rest of your life will be.

So even though you got up this morning and you felt the like nothing was different, you feel like you've accepted that you will never have highs again, you still feel like you're looking through fogged up glasses, and you're simply going through the motions, there's one thing to keep in mind.

You did get up.

And even though your world right now is that broken grey,

your vision is clouded, you homesickness has not been relieved, and your choking down more fucking tea to try and "naturally cure yourself", one day it won't feel that way. It might not be tomorrow, or next month, but eventually it will be one day. That day your eyes will be clear, your heart won't be heavy, and you'll find yourself reaching for an orange or a green while you order a coffee because why not.

You just have to keep getting up.

3

Read This If You're 23 And Lost

Heidi Priebe

So you're 23 and you have no idea what comes next.

First of all, congratulations. You're ahead of the game.

Do you know how long most people wait to realize that they're lost? Do you know many people never do? Do you understand how many people go through their entire lives aimlessly floundering; only to realize at the very end of it that none of what they did was what they wanted? It's a lot more than you'd think. And most of those people thought they had it all figured out at twenty-three.

After all, it's not so hard to be found when you are twenty-three years old. There are infinite hoards of people who will tell you what to do and where to go. There are endless opportunities for you to make money and prosper. All you have to do is let go of what you want for yourself. You just have to subscribe to living someone else's dream.

If you are lost at twenty-three, you are exactly where you need to be right now. I know that it is not where you would like — stuck in the middle of uncertainty and failure and your own inconsistent desires. I know it's not the place you thought you'd be when you screamed, "Cheers!" on your 20th birthday in anticipation of the next exciting decade. I know that you would rather be just about anywhere but here except you can't figure out where to go and it is driving you slowly up the wall. I know what it's like to be twenty-three and lost. I know that it's the worst place on earth.

But the fact that you are lost right now tells you something. It tells you that your life as it has been is not your life as it will be. It tells you that you're not the kind of person who settles for okay or sort of good enough. The fact that you are lost tells you that you would rather be living in the middle of uncertainty than dead-set on something that makes you consistently miserable. And I'm not sure if you realize how rare that really is. How few people still give a shit about doing something meaningful with their lives. How many more people we need who are just like you — lost and reeling, yet still pushing themselves to do better.

You are lost because you care. You're lost because you're passionate. You're lost because you know that there is more inside of you than what you're currently offering the world and that is a brilliant thing to know.

At 23, J.K. Rowling was broke. Tina Fey was working at the YMCA. Oprah had just gotten fired from her first job as a TV reporter and Walt Disney had declared bankruptcy. None of these wildly successful individuals could have predicted what was in store for them next but the one thing they all had in common was that they knew that there was more to them than what they were doing at the time. And that's what you have in common with them, too. You know that there's a bigger, better version of yourself to bring to life. You just haven't gotten there yet.

So let's look at where to go from here. If your life is lying splintered on the floor, which pieces do you want to pick up and keep? Which do you leave? What do you choose not to re-create now that you're given the chance to start over? Because that is exactly the chance that you have at twenty-three. You get to strip your life down to its bare bones and build the whole thing back up from scratch. It's not the easiest thing to do. But it's the best thing. The bravest thing. The most reward-ing thing and the kind of thing you only get the opportunity to do through being lost.

So right now, let yourself be a little bit lost. Because you don't get found by staying comfortable. You don't get found by running away. You don't get found by fighting your deepest impulses and you definitely don't get found by hiding out. You get found by doing exactly what it is that you are doing right now — which is delving right into the heart of your life and fighting like hell for what matters.

If you're never lost you never get found.

And you're the kind of person worth searching for.

4

Read This If You've Stopped Believing In Love

Heidi Priebe

Love doesn't start off difficult to believe in.

The first, even the second time you love someone, you're starry-eyed and openhearted. You rush into relationships with the unshakeable eagerness of a toddler trying their first solid food. You've been starved for real love all of your life and suddenly there it is — available to you in abundance!

So you give and you take and you want and you demand so much from those first few relationships. You want the love story you have been waiting for. You want the partner you truly deserve. You have a laundry list of everything you cannot wait to do, see, experience and become through loving someone else. You have so much to give! You have so much to receive!

If your expectations fail to be met, you just pretend and invent. Your first love story takes place largely inside your own mind and in many ways, you're fine with that. Even the falling apart of the relationship possesses a certain poetic tragedy. The good things cannot last forever and you know that. And so, you try again. You fall in love again. You hope again. You feel again. You have faith again, that this one is going to be it for real. And you repeat this process as many times as it takes.

Until somewhere along the line, something goes wrong. Something inside of you breaks in the place where it has always only bent and in a swift, unexpected instant, your heart falls cleanly apart.

The truth about these kinds of heartbreaks is that they don't bring the raw form of pain that you're used to. It's not the excruciating hurt, mind-numbing disbelief or short-lived anger that you're used to going through at the end of a relationship. It isn't a fiery, passionate emotion that you can empower yourself back from the brink of. It's something much quieter and subtler. It's the acceptance of the idea — from some deep place within you — that maybe love isn't what you thought it was.

That if you can fight that hard, for that long, with someone you care about that much and still have it all fall to pieces, maybe there isn't much left out there to hope for. Maybe love doesn't really conquer anything. Maybe it's all just some grandiose idea we made up to sell jewelry and distract ourselves from the painful realities of living. Maybe none of it was ever built to last.

It's like this quiet, certain part of you that believe in love for all of those years just packed up its bags and moved out in the middle of the night. You no longer feel guarded, apprehensive or excited about the prospect of meeting someone new. You just feel indifferent. You see the ending from the starting line and the race no longer seems to be worth running.

And the truth is, this happens to us all. Not a single one of us gets out of life with our hearts fully intact — we all have scrapes and jagged edges where the smooth parts used to be. Most of us have lost a love we thought would last forever. Most of us have felt disillusioned and spent. Most of us reached a point where we our hearts were too tired to keep going and we weren't sure what the point was in trying again.

But here's what you have to remember through those times when hope seems to be lost:

It's not love that you've stopped believing in. What you've stopped believing in is the specific vein of love that you have always been quick to identify — perhaps the kind you saw in movies or the kind that your first partner gave you. You've stopped believing in a lofty, idealistic form of love that was born of made-up stories you would tell yourself.

And now, all that's left is the real stuff.

Now that you've shaved away the fantasy and fairytale of how things were supposed to unfold, you can finally open yourself up to a quieter, realer version of love. One that doesn't impose or demand. One that doesn't expect or expand. One that takes things are they are — not as you imagine them to be — and works with that reality. That allows it the space to grow into something concrete.

In a way, we are all virgins of real love unless and until we first become jaded. Before this point, we were living in a fairytale of how we wanted love to be. And afterwards, we are offered the opportunity to accept love as it really exists: In all its flawed, imperfect glory.

And the beautiful part about that kind of love is that it doesn't require the lofty idealism we once possessed in order to continue to exist. Because that kind of love is based on truth. It's based on reality. It's based on whatever we choose to work long and hard to build alongside somebody else.

And that kind of love doesn't require us to believe in a thing.

5

Read This If You Think You're Finally Getting Your Sh*t Together

Ari Eastman

We are all spinning apart and it's starting to terrify us. That one friend who worshipped Kerouac and boasted never settling down now has a steady job and is getting married in the fall. The girl who used to hide empty vodka bottles in her bedroom closet has a baby. Everything is the same and changing all at once. "Where did the time go?" is a mantra we repeat at every gathering. "Where did the time go?"

We all go out and celebrate, raising glasses instead of red plastic cups and wonder if this is what growing up looks like. Someone spills wine all over their shirt and we all burst into laughter. Loud. That kind of laughter that you'd try to suppress in elementary school classes. You know this is grounds for getting in trouble. The teachers will surely yell, but your friend made that one face and now you're biting your lip to keep from snorting. Belly laughs. Abdominal contraction laughs.

We start counting back exes and hook ups. Some of us only

need one hand to do it. 5 fingers or less. Some of us need to use our toes. Our legs. Arms. All the limbs possible.

"Whatever happened to ____?"

"I heard he went into the air force."

"What about ____?"

"I actually have no clue."

We pull up cell phones and become millennial Sherlocks. We find profiles of people we had crushes on in elementary school and marvel at what they've turned into. Or grimace.

"Dodged a bullet with that one."

Someone goes home early because they have to wake up for work.

Someone goes home to their significant other.

Someone goes home to a baby or a dog or a fish they are weirdly invested in.

Someone goes home because they're just really tired.

"When did we stop being messes?" Someone asks. But we know the truth. Behind the jobs and 401(k)s and stable relationships, we are still those scared kids. Those beautifully lost kids. Those happy and confused kids trying to prove they are adults.

Growing up is a lot like that, I think. Convincing the world you've got it all figured out. Even when we know it's a lie. We're all still trying.

6

Read This If You've Ever Wanted To Die

Ari Eastman

On a drive home from Los Angeles, I hit that weird point in a solo road trip where one gets nostalgic as hell. It was the first time I'd successfully been in Los Angeles and not tried to contact him. *Progress*, I tell myself. *I think this is progress.*

Jeff Buckley's version of *Hallelujah* begins to play and the road gets a little blurry. Roads shouldn't really get blurry. I'd assume that's number one rule at the DMV – Hey, blurry road? Stop driving!

So I did.

I pulled off at the next exit and stopped. I stopped everything.

I didn't want to die or anything. That's not what it was. Yes, Hallelujah is a song that triggers a massive waterfall of tears (and if it doesn't for you, you sound like an Android, so kudos on that) and I was having ~*~emotions~*~ but not suicidal ones.

In fact, I was thinking the exact opposite. I was thankful to be alive. I was so grateful I didn't drive off a cliff like I'd fantasized about a year ago. I was so fucking *happy* that I stuck it out.

Because if I had died those times I thought I was permanently stuck in a black hole, this mess of sucking out any glimmer of hope and spitting it far away, I wouldn't have been here: sitting in my car feeling overwhelmed by how unbelievably appreciative I was.

Everyone thinks about dying. Sure, not everyone thinks about being the cause of their own death, but it's a subject we all think about sometimes. I used to be terrified of how easy death could come to people. As a child, I suffered from terrible insomnia because I would start thinking about eternal blackness and, shockingly enough, that doesn't equal nice, relaxing bedtime thoughts. And when you watch people you love die, the thought becomes a weird part of you.

I'm not afraid to say death is always tucked away in my mind somewhere. That's not to say I have suicidal thoughts always leaping out when I least expect it, but yes, dying is a thing I think about. Isn't it weird? That on one hand, I can become terrified of developing cancer and let WebMD convince me a bug bite is actually the start of a tumor. And then on the other, I stand at edges of cliffs and wonder what would happen if I jumped off.

Doesn't make much sense. But I guess life doesn't.

If you are struggling, I can't give you some magic formula or combination of words to immediately enlighten you with joy and puppies. That's just not how it works. And anyone who tells you there's just ONE simple step to your sudden eternal happiness is either lying to you or just totally unaware of how it feels to want everything to stop. I've been there. I've wanted to stop the clock. Forever.

For all the times I've wanted to die, I think about the times

I've laughed so hard my abdominal muscles felt sore and I woke up thinking, *What the hell? Did I go to the gym last night?*

For all the times I've wanted to die, I think about kissing new mouths or falling in love with someone and growing old. It would be an honor to gain wrinkles with someone. I want to age alongside someone and watch our bodies change together.

For all the times I've wanted to die, I think about my mother. And the thought, even if only temporarily, evaporates.

I hope you stick it out with us. I hope you aren't afraid to talk to someone and get help. Because getting help isn't a sign of weakness. It's a sign of self-reflection and intelligence. Not everyone is able to reach a place of understanding, and you have. You've realized something feels off. It hurts. It feels like you're alone on an island and there's no way you can ever swim back to society. But I think you can. I really do.

For all the times you wanted to die, but didn't, someone else did. But right now, I am grateful it wasn't you. I am so glad you are still here. Because being alone on that island isn't real isolation when you discover how many others are there too. Like some *Lost* sequel, we all got dumped onto this place and are trying to find a way off. And we will. But you've got to stay alive to do it. You've got to stay with us or the boat will never come.

7

Read This If You Are Fiercely Independent But Also Ridiculously Emotional

Marisa Donnelly

This is what it means to be independent: you make your own decisions, you stand on your own two feet, you pull yourself up when you fall down, and you have your sh*t together.

You have always been this way, always been okay on your own. You have never been afraid to go solo and to trust yourself. And you are continually looking for ways to be even more self-sufficient, to carve your own life path, to do what you want.

But you also love. And love terribly, beautifully, fully. You love with a passion that's sickening. A consuming, knotting, mess of emotion that interweaves you with another person. A love that twists your feelings, throws you upside-down, and makes you put your faith and stubbornness and fiercely-independent self in the hands of this other person.

Because of this, you live in a constant state of tension.

There are two things you want—to be your own person and

to love—but you want them just as equally. You crave that sense of self, the ability to not have to depend on anyone else for the life you want. But when you love, you mesh your life with another person's. Willingly. Happily. The path you have set for yourself becomes tangled with that person's. And this both thrills and terrifies you.

Your world then becomes an inner battle. You quiet your stubborn mind and give into love. You find yourself curling into this person's lap like a puppy, craving his touch, his kiss. Falling. You become the woman that confides in a man, the woman that leans on a man when she's feeling lost, the woman that thinks of this man equally, if not before, herself. This is beautiful. This is love.

But then you suddenly balk. You feel weak, dependent, breakable. You have become the woman that let a man in, who trusted him, who can easily be crushed by the same hands that touch her. So you swing to the other side. You pull away. You spend time alone, just recharging, remembering that sense of self. Letting go.

Neither side makes you fully happy. Neither side leaves you feeling complete. You cannot seem to find a balance because you crave both things so equally. And so you live in this place of tension—what you want and who you are, what you are becoming and yet so scared to be.

You are an independent woman. A woman with a strong heart and passionate soul. You cannot let go of that part of you, the part that decides for herself, finds strength in her ability to stand alone. Yet you cannot be afraid to love. You cannot be afraid to embrace that ridiculously emotional side of you, the side that blends your strength with your passion. The side that makes you whole.

You are not complete without both—without the strength you carry, without the tears and words and kisses you freely give. You are a strong woman. You are an emotional woman. You are a perfect mix of both.

8

Read This If You Thought You'd Be Further Along In Life By Now

Ari Eastman

So after Netflix asked, "Are you still watching?" one too many times, you decide to take a break from possible murderers, unrealistic romantic comedies, and undead creatures running amuck.

You end up on Facebook or Instagram — some social media site that helps us all keep tabs on our friends (or, more accurately, people we had two classes with in high school).

You scroll without a purpose; it's purely a habitual thing at this point. You see the smiling, shiny faces of people who have it *together*. Who get it. Who are, somehow, so ahead of you. And the ache sets in.

You thought you'd be so much further at this point.

You know it shouldn't be a competition, but Joey looks so happy and Carrie just bought her first home. All your childhood diaries filled with who you hoped you'd become still exist somewhere in the back of your mind. You pull up the catalogue on nights like this, when you decide to host a solo pity party and almost want to laugh/cry at how cliché you're being. And right now, it feels like it's you against the world.

It's you, lost and stumbling in the dark, against a world that has moved on.

But here's the thing, that's just not true.

We all occasionally feel as if we're inadequate in some aspect of our lives. Sometimes, it falls into a specific category: love, career, social, etc. And other times, *everything* feels a little lacking. Painfully human moments when damaging thoughts like, "What am I doing wrong?" creep in.

If you feel behind in life, I urge you to ask yourself, "What am I using as a measurement?"

Because quite frankly, this Milestone Marathon we think we're supposed to engage in is utter bullshit. It's almost guaranteed to leave one feeling like SOMEHOW they don't quite stack up, and rarely does it lead to productivity. You simply end up feeling more alone.

Oh, so a girl you haven't spoken to in four years just got engaged? Good for her, and her life. Which, reminder, is not YOUR life. That guy on your dorm floor who used to pass out in the common room every Friday night is now raking in over six figs? Again. Good. For. Him.

How are any of these people related to you? How do their successes (or calculated things you're being shown) have any influence on your life?

You think that if you haven't found your exact passions, your perfect career, or your clear-cut path you're not doing life *correctly*? Who says such a thing even exists?

Who are we even competing with?

Imagine you are 87 and old and wrinkly, and dying, you

think you're going to remember those innocuous posts you were jealous of?

Hell. No.

Everything has become so assumed. *This* is how you live. *This* is what someone your age should achieve. *This* is how you know you're doing it right.

You should aim to be kind. Aim to be compassionate. Aim to be understanding. Aim to allow and give love.

Everything else we've been brainwashed to believe we need. Take care of yourself. And that might mean a totally different life than one you've been told you should attain. Only you can figure it out. No manual, no outside advice.

Just survive. Life is about surviving the best way you know how.

9

Read This If You Don't Really Have An Eating Disorder, But Kind Of Do

Tatiana Pérez

"Have you ever starved yourself to lose weight?" the nurse asks.

"Sure," I shrug.

"Have you ever made yourself vomit to lose weight?"

"Not for a long time."

"Do you think your weight is too much, too little, or just right?"

I can hear my stomach grumbling as I shyly blurt out the obvious answer to her question: "too much." I binged on some bullshit organic Oreos last night, so I skipped breakfast.

She puts down her pen.

"Oh, honey…do you really think you're overweight?"

I feel proudly uncomfortable—she thinks I'm delusional, and that's a relief.

"Uhh…well, I don't think I'm fat, but yeah, I think I'm over-weight by own standards."

I'm 5'4" on a good day, and I weigh 126 pounds. I lied—sometimes, I really do think I'm fat.

I don't have an eating disorder, and technically, I never have. But have I had something like it? Yeah. I know very few women who haven't.

Rewind.

It's summer of 2008. I just finished eighth grade.

I tearily surf the web to find a bottle of some bogus green tea diet pills my friend Molly recommended. I'm the skinniest I've ever been. I've shed the remainder of the baby fat that's haunted me since I was old enough to look in the mirror and hate what I saw—since I was seven or eight, I think. But, just a few hours ago, I cried in a Victoria's Secret fitting room as I tried on a bikini that exposed my imaginary love handles. So the pills are a must.

I pull at all the "problem spots" on my pre-pubescent body as I scroll through Thinspiration—this blog Molly showed me that boasts pictures of stick-thin girls whose image we can aspire to. I try to make myself throw up the breakfast burrito I half-ate seven hours ago, but nothing comes out. Usually, nothing comes out. I let out a soft cry of frustration before updating my weight loss goals:

- Stomach: 8 pounds
- Thighs: 4 pounds each
- Arms: 2 pounds each
- Face: 1/2 pounds

I want to weigh 80 pounds. I want to be so thin that my mom will ask if I'm OK. Then, I'll be beautiful.

Four years later, and it's spring of 2012. I'm a senior in high school.

I anxiously scroll through Facebook photos of a kind-of friend I saw at a party last night. She just lost 20 pounds in two weeks following her "priet"—prom diet. We're all prieting too, so she readily divulged how she'd done it:

"Cocaine and coffee, of course."

I don't do drugs, but if I did, I wouldn't *have to* have hard-boiled eggs for dinner after almost passing out in a 90-minute hot yoga class.

Three years later, and it's summer again—this time, I'm 21-years-old, and the year's 2015.

My doctor enters to give me my physical. Concerned by my survey responses, she asks me how I lost almost 20 pounds since last summer. This time, I don't lie.

"Months of too much exercise, followed by months of no exercise, followed by months of a little exercise, and a lot less food. I don't make myself throw up or anything…I just have a complicated relationship with my body, I guess."

It's true. Our relationship is fucked up. Always has been. And many women—most women—can relate.

I've never been anorexic or bulimic. I've never been too thin, because I could never pull it off. But me and 9 outta 10 of the women I love? We might not have textbook eating disorders—and, really, I don't mean to reduce the painful reality of those who do—but we know what it feels like, I think.

We know what it feels like to be incapacitated by body

obsession—by food thoughts. Because we've long been slaves to that apex of tall, thin, white, blond perfection. That apex we've been climbing to since we were old enough to look in the mirror and hate what we saw—since we were old enough to be consumed by our consumption. To jitter with paranoia that people are constantly critiquing our bodies—cheapening them. Fattening them. To fiercely hold the fucked up belief that our weight and our happiness are perfectly, inversely proportional. Even if we've never had an eating disorder, we grew up with them.

That's why a violent surge of panic rushes through me when my boss suggests we order pizza for dinner. I had two slices of bread with my salad at lunch—that's *plenty* of carbs for today.

That's why I wake up feeling so damn disgusting after I have a fat post-midnight snack. I have a hard and fast rule: no eating after 12. Because I want food to be a thing of my before-midnight yesterday—not a thing of my after-midnight tomorrow.

That's why I still avoid eye contact with my boyfriend while I'm getting undressed. He loves my body—he says so. But I don't really believe him. It's soft where it should be hard and bloated where it should be flat. He's seen better bodies. Mine's not so good.

And that's why a small, secret part of me still wishes I weighed 80 pounds. That's why a small, secret part of me still wishes I was so thin that my mom would ask me If I was OK. Because then, I'd be beautiful.

But I'm wrong. We're all wrong. And, really, we're already beautiful.

10

Read This If You're 25 And You Have Nothing To Show For It

Kim Quindlen

Everybody else around you has it together, regardless of what they're doing. Whether they're in finance or publishing or education, they know what they want, and you don't. They have a great job that they love, or they're engaged or married or pregnant and starting a family. They're traveling and exploring the world and taking vacations that they can afford. They have careers or spouses or babies, and you have nothing. They're doing everything, while you watch from the ground. Or at least, it seems that way.

It seems like you're the only 25-year-old in the entire world that has no clue where they are supposed to go from here. And while you make jokes with your friends about how your life is a mess and how you don't know what you're doing, your laughter is hollow. Because at the end of the day, it's not really that funny to you anymore. You don't know where the last five years went and you cannot comprehend the fact that you're now halfway through your twenties and you have nothing to show for it.

Twenty and *twenty-one* are a joke. You're in college, you're drunk all the time, your biggest concern is whether or not you're going to see your ex at the next house party. *Twenty-two* is overwhelming but full of potential. You're out in the real world, but it's still cushioned enough that you feel you have room to try new things and behave like a college student on the weekends. *Twenty-three* is when the pressure starts to set in, but you still feel this lightness around you, this strong sense of hope, this belief that the world is still at your fingertips because you're still *so, so* young. Then comes *twenty-four*, when you're trying to mold your mind into that of an adult, while telling yourself that in a year from now, it will all make sense.

And then *twenty-five* hits and nothing makes sense. You start to resent people. You resent your friend with the cool marketing job, and the other friend who's planning a wedding with a wonderful fiancé, even though you know they've done nothing wrong. You're more so resenting the fact that you're not in their place. You wish that stuff was happening to you. You wish there was some marked out path for you to follow that would tell you what you're supposed to do and when, because it seems like there was an actual path marked out for everyone except you.

It would be fun to write a post saying *Screw all them, they're settling down and are bored and are missing out on all of the fun you're having. You're figuring out what life is all about, you're exploring on your own, and they're just wasting their twenties being boring old adults.*

But that would be a lie. Because there is no right way to live out your twenties. There are some people who were married by twenty-two and wouldn't have it any other way, because they're happy and in love and building the foundation of a life with another person. There are some people who discovered their dream job right out of college and just happen to love what they do while still having an amazing salary. That doesn't make them wrong. Enviable, perhaps, but not wrong.

It's tempting to try to find a way to think of yourself as mentally or emotionally superior to them — to tell yourself that you're having *life experiences* while they sit at home being old and lame. But that's just your ego talking, trying to keep you above water so that you feel like you can breathe amongst all these other twenty-five-year-olds who seem more successful than you.

Here's what it comes down to. It's okay to be twenty-five and have nothing to show for it, as long as you never lose that thirst for life and that desire to keep working hard and searching for what it is that you want to do. You're not going to find true, genuine happiness and fulfillment through a career or a lifestyle or another person — but those things can certainly help you along the way. They can certainly contribute to your search to find your true meaning and purpose.

There's no right way to be twenty-five. Because there's no one, single, specific way to be human. As long as you keep your eyes open, as long as you keep trying new things and working hard and refusing to accept mediocrity as your fate, you will be okay. You will be happy. You will be exactly where you're supposed to be.

11

Read This If You're Having Doubts About Your Relationship

Mélanie Berliet

When you love someone madly, the last thing you expect is to entertain doubts about the strength of your bond. Questioning seems contrary to commitment. Even if you do so privately, inside your own mind—in the midst of a sleepless night, while jogging, or showering—it can feel like a serious betrayal.

After reaching a certain point, you don't want to question whether your partner's values are aligned with yours enough to move forward, long past the lustful stage and into lasting romantic attachment, or whether you want the same things out of life in practical, realistic terms, or whether you can imagine parenting together and growing old alongside each other, eventually dying hand-in-hand as you've discussed so many times while caught in the throws of passion. You don't want to let yourself ask these questions because it seems disrespectful to the person you love and the life you've built together so far.

But you must—without freaking out, if possible. Because

if you don't, those pesky questions will eat at you from the inside out until your heart is Swiss cheese, compromising your capacity to love.

No matter how strongly you feel about your significant other, it's natural to feel confused about the relationship once in a while. You might doubt the fact that the person you love loves you as much as they claim to. You might doubt that your partner is worthy of the trust you've placed in them. You might wonder if you can make it as a couple long-term. Especially in matters of the heart, none of us is all-knowing.

Pangs of uncertainty can sprout up for no good reason, tickling your consciousness and begging for attention no matter how unjustified they may be. On other occasions, your gut may respond to blatant signs of trouble, or to subtle but significant cues. Unfortunately, it's tough to know the difference. But it's always worth trying to decipher the root cause of whatever doubts creep up. You can't fear the outcome of addressing them too much to deny yourself the room to figure things out. However unpleasant the process may be, confronting uncertainty is the only way to return to a point of clarity.

You may have reason to doubt your relationship, and you may not. You may decide that the woman or man you've long thought of as "the one" is exactly right for you after all, or not. You may choose to do the work to repair whatever aspects of your relationship are broken, or deem the situation a lost cause. Relationship doubts aren't necessarily an indicator of insurmountable problems, but they can be. The morning you wake up wondering whether the person next to you belongs there, you're not doomed to split. But you might.

So listen yourself, but with the utmost caution. Don't ignore your inner voices, but don't become a victim of your own speculative thoughts, either. Be as reasonable as your emotions will allow. Seek counsel from friends and family members, but don't assume their insights are more accurate than yours. Get therapy from a trained professional, but avoid horoscopes and psychics. Cyberstalk your boyfriend, girlfriend, husband, or wife all you want, but never *ever* cybersnoop. (If you don't know the difference, figure it out.) Entertain every possibility—leaving, cheating, moving, ransacking the apartment, draining the bank account—but understand the distinction between thinking, saying, and *doing* something. Unless you're a saint who only thinks pure, saintly thoughts, don't feel obligated to express every theory or view that crosses your mind. Complete transparency isn't as healthy as it sounds, and we're all responsible to a certain extent for protecting each other from our own minds. That doesn't mean you can't communicate openly and honestly, but it does mean that you should choose your words carefully, especially when speaking to the person you love.

Ultimately, whether you have reason to be suspicious or paranoid or hesitant—whether you and your significant other stay together, or break up—you will both be fine. Love is painful and confounding and exhausting and frustrating and overwhelmingly awesome. It leads us to places we treasure, and to places we abhor. It brings out the absolute best and worst in us. Love demands navigating sharp curves, steep hills, and some impossibly giant potholes. The terrain is uneven—and that's okay. If it were simple or easy, it wouldn't be so damn hard to find, nurture, or let go of. But no one's ever died of a broken heart.

People grow apart because individuals evolve, often separately. But relationships evolve, too. If you stay together, your love will be no weaker for the questions you once pondered. On the contrary, without a doubt, you'll be stronger as a couple.

12

Read This If There's Someone You Can't Forgive

Heidi Priebe

I hate every cliché that exists about forgiveness.

I know every adage, every piece of advice, every regularly endorsed opinion on the topic because I've scoured my way through the literature. I've read every blog post about letting go of anger. I've written down Buddha quotes and stuck them on post-its to my wall. I know that no part of it is simple. I know the adages are tired. I know the gap between "Deciding to forgive" and actually feeling peace can seem entirely unbridgeable. I know.

Forgiveness is a vast, un-traversable land for those of us who crave justice. The very thought of letting someone walk away scot-free from what they've done makes us sick. We don't want to simply wipe our hands clean. We want to transfer the blood onto to theirs. We want to see the scores evened and the playing field leveled. We want them to bear the weight of what they've done, not us.

Forgiveness seems like the ultimate betrayal of yourself. You don't want to give up the fight for justice after what has happened to you. The anger is burning inside you and pumping toxicity throughout your system. You know that, but you can't let it go. The anger is as inseparable a part of you as your heart or mind or lungs. I know the feeling. I know the second heartbeat that is fury.

But here's the thing about anger: it's an instrumental emotion. We stay angry because we want justice. Because we think it's useful. Because we assume that the angrier we are, the more change we will be capable of incurring. Anger doesn't realize that the past is over and the damage has been done. It tells you that vengeance will fix things. It's on the pursuit of justice.

Except the justice we want isn't always realistic. Staying angry is like continually picking the scab off a cut because you think that if you keep the wound open, you won't get a scar. It's thinking that someday, the person who wronged you can come give you stitches with such incredible precision that you'll never know the cut was once there. The truth about anger is that it's nothing more than the refusal to heal, because you're scared to. Because you're afraid of who you'll be once your wounds close up and you have to go on living in your new, unfamiliar skin. You want your old skin back. And so anger tells you to keep that wound bleeding.

When you're seething, forgiveness seems impossible. We want to be capable of it, because intellectually we know it's the healthiest choice to make. We want the peace forgiveness offers. We want the release. We want the madness in our brains to quiet down, and yet we cannot find a way to get there.

Because here's what they all fail to tell you about forgiveness: It's not going to fix anything. It's not an eraser that will wipe away the pain of what's happened to you. It does not undo the pain that you've been living with and grant you immediate peace. Finding peace is a long, uphill battle. Forgiveness is just what you take to stay hydrated along the way.

Forgiveness means giving up hope for a different past. It means knowing that the past is over, the dust has settled and the destruction left in its wake can never be reconstructed to resemble what it was. It's accepting that there's no magic solution to the damage that's been caused. It's the realization that as unfair as the hurricane was, you still have to live in its city of ruins. And no amount of anger is going to reconstruct that city. You have to do it yourself.

Forgiveness means accepting responsibility — not for causing the destruction, but for cleaning it up. It's the decision that restoring your own peace is finally a bigger priority than disrupting someone else's.

Forgiveness doesn't mean you have to make amends with who hurt you. It doesn't mean befriending them, sympathizing with them or validating what they have done to you. It just means accepting that they've left a mark on you. And that for better or for worse, that mark is now your burden to bear. It means you're done waiting for the person who broke you to come put you back together. It's the decision to heal your own wounds, regardless of which marks they're going to leave on your skin. It's the decision to move forward with scars.

Forgiveness isn't about letting injustice reign. It's about creating your own justice, your own karma and your own destiny. It's about getting back onto your feet and deciding that the rest of your life isn't going to be miserable because of what happened to you. It means walking bravely into the future, with every scar and callous you've incurred along the way. Forgiveness means saying that you're not going to let what happened to you define you any longer.

Forgiveness doesn't mean that you are giving up all of your power. Forgiveness means you're finally ready to take it back.

13

Read This If You're Worried That You'll Never Find 'The One'

Heidi Priebe

Imagine something crazy for me, quickly.

What if you peered into a fortune ball right now — this very second, today — and saw with indisputable clarity that you were never going to meet the love of your life?

That's a sad thing that I'm asking you to think of, I'm aware. You've been hoping to meet "The One" for a while now — or at least someone half-decent who you can deal with for the rest of your life. I know, I know. You're not fanciful like everyone else. You don't believe in soul mates. But you were expecting to meet someone you liked a fair amount. Someone to curl up next to at the end of a long day, who would take care of you when you got sick and listen to your stories every evening after work. We all hope that. We're human.

But imagine for a second that you knew — with 100% certainty — that you were never going to meet that person. What about your life would that knowledge change?

Because here's the thing about finding love — it affects us constantly. And we all loathe admitting it. But love is on the forefront of our actions even when it's not on the forefront of our minds. It's the reason you bought those new jeans last week. It's the reason you went to that barbecue that you didn't want to go to last weekend. It's the reason you sometimes feel cripplingly insecure and inadequate and scared about everything that's coming next. Love's what inspires most of your greatest changes.

So if you knew, with indisputable certainty, that love was never going to be yours, how would you live your life differently? What about your daily routine would you alter? What about your long-term plans?

Your first inclination may be to say "Nothing." After all, you're a smart person. You have plans that don't involve someone else's influence. We all do. But ponder it a few moments more. Because here's what we don't want to admit about love: it is a crutch that we use all the time. The idea that someday somebody will love all our flaws is a subtle excuse not to work on them. The principle of two halves making a whole restrains us from becoming our own better half. We want someone to swoop in during our darkest hour and save us, but what if we knew they never would? We'd have to start doing everything differently.

If you knew that love would never be an option for you, what would be? How would you structure the rest of your life? Would it have a heavier focus on career, a stronger inclination toward success? Or would you use the time to invest in yourself — go on a few more vacations, travel further outside your comfort zone? If you knew that you would never again feel the rush of budding romance, where would you turn to for your thrills? How would you get your blood pumping?

And what about your other relationships — would they suddenly take on more weight? Would you spend more time appreciating your family, if you knew that they are the people who will have loved you the most strongly at the end of your life? What about your friendships? Would you nurture and care more for the people who love you platonically if you knew that nobody would ever love you romantically? Would you show up a little more often, share a little more of your life?

My inclination is to believe that never finding love would be a game-changer for most of us. One we'd initially consider to be devastating but may eventually realize is the ultimate liberation. Without the fear of ending up alone, the opportunities open to you would become endless. You could live on every continent. You could scale the corporate ladder. You could go back to school and get that degree you've always felt interested in, without worrying about the financial burden your debt may place on somebody else. Love holds us back in an infinite amount of subtle ways that perhaps we do not even realize. And the guarantee of its absence may just be the ultimate sense of liberation.

Because if we didn't have to search for the love of our lives, we would finally be free to realize that we are allowed to be the loves of our own. That we can spend our lives developing ourselves, challenging ourselves, pampering ourselves and building ourselves up to be bigger, more capable people than we ever once hoped to become. We could become everything we've been searching for. We could construct our soul mates in ourselves.

If there's one thing we all need to stop doing, it's waiting around for someone else to show up and change our lives. Just be the person you've been waiting for. Live your life as if you are the love of it. Because that's the only thing you know for sure — that through every triumph, every failure, every fear and every gain that you will ever experience until the day you die, you are going to be present. You are going to be the person who shows up to accept your rewards. You are going to be the person who holds your own hand when you're broken. You are going to be the person who gets yourself up off the floor every time you get knocked down and if those things are not love-of-your-life qualities, I don't know what are.

We have to start appreciating all that we bring to our own lives. Because the ironic truth is, you are most attractive when you're not worried about who you're attracting. When you're living your life confidently, freely and without restraint, you emit the kind of energy that it just isn't possible to fake. The kind of energy that's capable of transforming not just your own life, but the lives of people around you.

So stop looking for The One to spend the rest of your life with. Be The One.

And let everybody else come searching for you.

14

Read This If You're Debating Whether Or Not To Go Out Tonight

Heidi Priebe

There will always be an infinite number of good reasons to stay in at night.

Because the party seems lame. Because you're tired after a long week of work. Because the possibility of this night turning into one that you talk about for months or years to come seems so impossibly small and you're done being tirelessly optimistic about it all. Nothing new ever happens and nobody interesting ever shows up and you can see how it's all going to end before it even begins. So you might as well stay home. You might as well relax into what you can be sure will be another mediocre night in your apartment. You have Netflix. And that's all you need.

There's nothing wrong with staying in now and then. We all need our down time and we all need our space. But the problem is when it becomes a pattern. Staying in. Checking out. Choosing certainty over uncertainty and forgetting to let chance into our lives.

We want excitement but we never seem to want to leave

the house. We want change but we can't be bothered changing from pajamas. We want lives that are varied and full but we choose comfort at each opportunity. We blame our lives for staying stagnant. And we blame them from the comfort of our living room couch.

I'm not arguing that one night out is going to turn your whole life around — not at all. I've been out enough times to know how it will go — your friend Shannon will drag you out to that party. You'll be the only single person there. You'll pour a drink, refrain from outwardly scowling and count the hours until you can retire. Worst-case scenario, you'll be trapped in the corner talking to someone's mind-numbing cousin named Anne. Best-case scenario, you will spend an hour talking to some impossibly cute guy named Jimmy whose girlfriend is working tonight. Shannon will take home her boyfriend. You will take home yourself.

It takes more than one night for your life to start happening. But here's the thing: It takes that first party where you don't know anyone to get to the party where you do. It takes that first forced conversation with a stranger to start the process of making a new friend. It takes more than one or two nights where you're grumpy and out of your comfort zone to build a life that fully thrives inside of it. You can't avoid those necessary evils. Not if you want to build a life that doesn't take place entirely between the confines of your own apartment. Not if you want it to progress.

Because here's the thing about those little interactions that seem so arbitrary — they resurface when you least expect it.

Maybe eight months from now you're out of work. Maybe Shannon posts a "Help Wanted" ad to your Facebook wall.

Maybe Anne sees it. Maybe she knows someone who's looking to hire in your field. Maybe in that half hour of dull conversation you shared over lukewarm beer, she learned something about you that impressed her. Maybe she scores you that interview. Maybe it lands you the job.

Maybe two years from now you're sitting in a coffee shop trying to sort out a project from work and Jimmy walks in and you both give each other that quizzical 'Don't I know you' head tilt. Maybe he approaches your table and after a few moments of fumbling awkwardly through possible mutual friends, you both proclaim, "Shannon," and share a knowing laugh. Maybe he pulls up a chair. Maybe he tells you about what he's been up to and the beautiful girlfriend doesn't seem to be in the picture. Maybe he gets your number. Maybe four dates later he doesn't feel like much of a stranger anymore.

Maybe no single night turns our lives around. Maybe nine times out of ten, we do nothing exciting, meet no one important and make no memories that are really worth remembering. But maybe one out of ten times we do.

Maybe one time out of ten we meet someone extraordinary. Maybe one time out of ten we stumble across a new opportunity. Maybe one out of every ten times we go home with starry eyes and open hearts after a truly incredible night with the people who honestly matter. And maybe that one time makes each of the nine duds before it seem worthwhile. Makes us glad we pushed through. Makes us glad we didn't pack it in at quiet night number seven.

Chances are, this won't be the best night of your life. Chances are you'll come home at midnight, vaguely angry that you wasted the last of your lipstick and consumed 500 calories of beer that you cannot get back. But that's the thing about your life — it isn't meant to be a series of instant gratifications. It builds on itself and that building happens slowly. It happens each time we say 'Yes' when we'd honestly rather say 'No.'

Maybe your life won't explode into beautiful, untamed chaos by the time the clock strikes 12 but maybe it doesn't have to. Maybe each night is not an end in itself but a small stepping stone that eventually moves you toward a bigger, better life. One that is fuller and richer and wilder than you ever expected it to be, because you kept welcoming change in, even when it seemed easier not to.

We think that one night isn't enough to make a difference — but we're wrong.

One night might make a whole world of difference.

But it definitely won't if you spend it alone on your couch.

15

Read This If You're Trying To Decide Whether Or Not They're Right For You

Heidi Priebe

There's a very specific method I like to use when I'm trying to decide whether or not someone's worth dating.

First, I sit down and think — long and hard — about every single trait that I desire in a potential partner.

I debate the pros and cons of various possible professions. I determine the importance of family ties. I consider whether I a chiseled jawline or a soft, forgiving smile and exactly how many inches taller or shorter I'd like them to be in comparison to myself. I research the components of long-lasting partnership. I consider how they'd measure up. I consult with friends and coworkers and eventually sit down to write a long, exhaustive list of exactly whom I'd like to end up with.

Then I decide whether or not to pursue the relationship based on how badly he or she makes me want to rip up the list.

Here's the thing when it comes to finding love: There is no

formula for it. And if there were, it would be a whole lot easier to manage. We'd date someone if they meet a list of ten or twenty ideal criteria. We'd reject them based on a list of 'red flag' items. We'd never have to wonder if someone was right or wrong with us because the answer would be written all over the facts and the decision would be simple as that.

And yet it's not as simple as that. Instead, we find ourselves deliberating endlessly.

He's really nice but I'm not nuts about his friends.

She's cute and funny but her room is kind of messy.

We weigh lists of pros and cons like they are the be-all end-all of our love lives and we're still never sure who to commit to.

Until, all of a sudden, we are.

Because here's what's too easy to forget when you've been mating and dating and deliberating for years to no avail: The right person will defy each pro and con.

The right person won't make you wonder. They won't make you deliberate. They won't make you grimace at a sheet of pre-determined qualities like, "Neatly trimmed facial hair," and "Must have read all Harry Potter books." They'll make you want to turn a new page. Start a new chapter. And write a list all about them.

Must have their exact smile. Their exact charm. Their exact job, their exact family, their exact personality and their exact quirks. The quirks you'd hate in absolutely anyone else. The quirks that are ironically what you love most about them.

They might be two inches two short. In an outlandishly strange profession. Abhorrent of dogs, excessively bearded and entirely unable to pronounce "Hermione" or "Voldemort." And yet for you, that will suddenly be perfect. You will relish the chance to wear flats, learn about their strange job, fall asleep in their haphazard bedroom and re-watch the *Harry Potter* movies. Your list will be an afterthought. The strange, unconventional nuances of everything they are will be the new 'must haves.'

We forget that in the busy, bustling world full of indifferent people who are only ever half-right for us, there could be one or two who are so inexplicably wonderful for us that we couldn't possibly have made them up. That the way they make us feel makes every 'con' on our list seem disposable. That the work we put in will be infinitely, inarguably worthwhile. That not trying with everything in it to make the relationship work won't be an option. That indifference will not make the radar.

And when you meet someone like that, you'll realize that what you've been doing all along has been a futile, pointless game. Because the truth of the matter is, if you have to wonder whether or not they're right for you, they're probably not.

If they were right, you wouldn't need a list. You wouldn't need to deliberate. You wouldn't need to weigh the pros and cons, carefully mark out your options and determine whether or not they would fit neatly into your life.

With the right person, you would know.

You'd know that the unchecked boxes can be altered. That the criteria they're missing doesn't matter. That whatever it takes to fit them into your life, you'll make work.

Because as the most infuriating of all happy couples like to claim, *when you know, you know.*

And until then, you just keep searching.

16

Read This If Your Relationship Has An Expiration Date

Heidi Priebe

I can't honestly recall a single relationship I've been in that didn't have an expiration date.

Some of these dates were inherent — the boys I met working at summer camps, the relationships I formed on the road. Those expirations were blatant and overt — on the 21st of April, one of us had a plane to get on. On the 30th of August, we all had to pack up our bags and go home.

Those end dates were the sweetest kind, if possible. They made everything before them seem heightened — every kiss more intense, every uttered word more special. There were no bruises to the ego upon parting — just a simple sinking feeling and the knowledge that life would go on. You got to hold on to the notion that there was one more person in the world whom you loved or adored or at the very least liked for a while. They were comforting, those expirations. They were a simple way of flirting with love.

The hardest expiration dates are not the overt ones though. The hardest expiration dates are the covert ones. The doubts that creep into your mind six months into a relationship. The arguments you simply can't resolve. The conversation you have about the future that keeps you up at night, turning over somebody's words inside your mind. These are the signs that point toward your inevitable destruction — the signals that indicate the end.

It works now, You remind yourself, *But he or she wants to live in the suburbs. They hate travel. They want (or they do not want) kids.*

And no matter how much you re-iterate to yourself that it doesn't matter or that you can cross that bridge when you come to it, it matters. It worries you. It encapsulates you. It makes you wonder if your relationship exists on borrowed time, if it's all going to come crashing down.

And if it's going to, when?

And if it's going to, shouldn't you just get out now?

We are obsessed with rescuing ourselves from pain. If something won't last forever, we'd rather knock it down early. Cut our losses. Save ourselves from falling from greater heights later on in the game.

We forget that the worth of everything is not measured by its longevity. That some of the best things simply don't last forever. After all, all of our favourite novels, movies and stories had endings. And yet, we read them anyway. We watched them anyway. We loved and learned from them anyway. They still had value, even though they eventually ended. And so do our relationships with people.

The uniquely beautiful thing about relationships that have expiration dates is that they aren't moving toward an end. They aren't about the future so they get to be about the now.

About every day you have left with that person. About everything they can teach you before life inevitably tears you apart. Because you know that someday, it is going to.

Someday you're going to wake up and they won't be asleep in bed beside you. Someday you'll hear a joke they'd love and not have their number to text it to. Someday you're going to need their advice and they will not be there to give it. And so you do the only thing that you can: You ask them now. You laugh with them now. You fall asleep beside them now, and relish every moment that you have before it's gone.

Relationships with expiration dates teach us that love doesn't have to last forever to be meaningful. That someone doesn't have to stick around to make an impact. That the best things in life are not always measured by their longevity but by their intensity. Their complexity. By their patience and wisdom and by every way our lives change as a result of them.

We don't get to hold onto every person we love in our lives. But we do get to decide whether or not we're going to appreciate them for everything they're worth while we have them.

And if we can learn to do that, then perhaps we'll find we can experience the most sincere form of love that exists. The kind that opens us up, takes our entire life by storm and then gently, quietly, teaches us how to let go.

And to appreciate what we have for as long as we get to hold onto it.

17

Read This If You've Never Been In Love

Tatiana Pérez

Five months ago, like anyone who's never been in love, part of me thought I was unlovable—because I wanted love badly, and I couldn't reconcile why I hadn't fallen in it yet.

Because five months ago, like anyone who's never been in love, I thought love was something you fall into—something that happens to you and that you can't stop or quiet or control—because that's what people who've never been in love think love is: quicksand.

Five months ago, I started sleeping with a boy. Five months ago, I'd never been in love.

He was a senior two weeks out of a two-year relationship, and I was a junior who wanted a boyfriend she'd never had and was sure she wouldn't find in college—and for those reasons, I was confident it wouldn't last. He was just another boy who wouldn't be able to handle me—just another boy I wouldn't want to love (or to love me).

The first night we slept together, we stayed up till 6 a.m. and didn't touch. He asked me if I'd ever done that—if I'd ever slept in a (straight) boy's bed without touching him. I said I had—I don't know why I lied. I guess I already liked him and wanted to play it cool. I guess we'd just become friends a few weeks before and I didn't want to make shit weird with this guy I thought was fucking funny and *cool*, since I don't find a lot of those. That night, we made up a religion. I can't tell you what it's about, because it's a religion only the two of us can know. That night, he made me feel like a kid. A few weeks later, he told me that *I* made him feel like a kid—I think that's still the best compliment he's ever given me.

It was intense, that touchless first night. We've never really talked about it, and I don't know if he agrees—but for me, it was intense.

The night after that, we slept together again. We stayed up till 6 a.m. again, till we almost didn't touch—again. But then, around 6:01, we started to touch.

He has this lucky stone he once found on a beach that he can't live without—he calls it his rock. We'd played with the rock all night, using it, I think, as some tiny basin for the ~sexual tension~ that'd been building for 24 hours. He started to touch me, with the rock, on my stomach. It was very intense. We've never really talked about it, and I don't know if he agrees—but for me, it was very intense.

That night, we just made out. I think that was the most fun I'd ever had with a (straight) boy, just making out. I must have known I liked him after that second night.

Five months ago, like anyone who's never been in love, I didn't know what love feels like...but I was pretty sure I'd know it when I'd found it.

Five months ago, like anyone who's never been in love, I thought "I love you" would be the fullest words I could possibly hear, in sequence, from a boy I loved, too.

Five months ago, I did not think *this* boy would be *that* boy.

I hadn't seen him for two weeks, and I missed him, even though I was newly confident that I didn't want a relationship with him. I'd asked him for one—for a relationship—when I was leaving him behind for summer while he was leaving me behind for grad week 'n' stuff. We'd see each other in New York in less than a month and I knew he wanted to be with me, but he still wouldn't give it to me—he wouldn't promise me exclusivity. He was too fiercely wedded to that false concept of independence founded on technical non-commitment to see what we had and to call it what it was—we'd had *the conversation* before, but this time, I thought, "If he doesn't see *us*, I'm done. I don't want this."

I still wanted him, you see, but I didn't want *this*. I decided I could keep seeing him while I started to see other guys, largely because, as I suspected, he was up to no good while we were apart—I'll spare you the details (really, I'll spare him the details—I know he's reading this, lol), but when he came clean, I wasn't surprised. I was, however, fucking *furious*...until, a few hours later, I wasn't. I was kind of furious at myself, honestly, for not staying furious, but I couldn't help it—I wasn't mad.

I should've known then that I loved him. Because it was painful, but I weirdly understood, and I felt weirdly unthreatened. It was like all his flaws and all my insecurities evaporated the moment he told me the truth—not just that he'd fucked up, but that he was deeply sorry he had. That he'd been mindless, and that he wanted to be with me. And just like that, I wanted to be with him again, too.

I don't know exactly when I started to suspect that, against all odds, I might be wrong—that, maybe, *this* boy was *that* boy. But I think it was then—about a month ago, right around the time this boy became my first boyfriend (oops!).

I remember kissing him goodbye one average mid-June morning and wanting to say it—"I love you." I'd never felt (and had to fight) that semi-overwhelming urge. I'd never been in love, so I wasn't sure what it meant, but I decided, then, that if I wanted say it, I probably felt it.

But, like anyone who's never been in love, I was too scared to take that plunge first. So I waited. In reality—just like I'd known he wanted to be with me—I knew he loved me already, but I was mildly terrified that he'd follow the same "if I don't say it, it's not real" principle he'd applied to our relationship for so long. So I waited.

I'm shit at waiting.

A few days ago, he interrupted ~stuff~ to breathily say, "I like you." Lol. I'd heard this before—many times. It was late and I was drunk. I responded, "do you love me?" He responded, "what does that mean?"

Groan.

"I don't know, dude. I've never been in love—I don't know."

But I did know, now. Because now, I was pretty sure I was no longer *anyone who's never been in love.*

The next day over FaceTime, he brought it up—that "serious question" I'd asked him the night before. He asked me again if I knew what love was. This time, I was sober and forward:

"Well, I don't know for sure, but here's what I *do* know: I've wanted to say it to you—I've felt unnervingly compelled to tell you I love you. I also know that, one day, we'll break up. That's kind of fucked up to say, I guess, but it's okay—we'll break up, because no matter how much I like you, I'm 21, and at this point, I'm pretty sure I'm not spending the rest of my life with you. But when I think about us, I see us together far in the future. I see us, maybe, finding each other again ten years from now and then, maybe, staying together. And I don't usually think that way. To me, that feels real."

The next night, in person, he told me he loves me.

I said it back, and it feels right. It feels like we've given what we've been feeling a name—it feels like we've just made what we've been feeling real.

So far, nothing's changed. I don't feel like I've fallen—I don't feel like I'm in quicksand. I feel like I've consciously, steadily *walked* into love. I feel like I've finally found someone who can handle me without ever trying to manage me. I feel like I've finally found someone whose flaws—and, trust, he has a lot of those—I don't resent. Someone whose flaws I embrace more readily than I do my own. Someone who makes me laugh. Someone who's smart in all the ways I find important. Someone who's fucking *fun*. Someone who motivates me to be a better version of me. And someone who loves me, I think, for all the reasons I've always wanted someone to love me—someone who loves what *I* love about me.

I believe desperately in the power of language. Things are nothing until we use words to to describe them, because that which language has not named does not exist.

And love, like anything, exists only if you *will it*, with words, *to* exist. When you tell someone you love them, you give what's happening a name. That's what makes it real—that's how you know you're in love.

18

Read This If You're Disappointed With The People Around You

Heidi Priebe

So the people around you let you down.

I'm sorry that you are going through that. I really am. There are few feelings more frustrating than being unsupported when you need support most. Than reaching out and having no one respond. Than slowly falling apart and having nobody around to help keep you together.

I'm sorry that you're feeling disappointment because it's an umbrella term for an array of greater agonies. But here's the truth about disappointment that we all loathe to acknowledge: It has very little to do with whoever let us down. Disappointment is entirely a construction of our own expectations. And no matter how many promises someone else made us, reality has no responsibility to comply with our expectations.

The problem with other people is that they're never going to understand us as intricately as we understand ourselves. We grow disappointed in the people around us because we use our own definition of love to measure what they are giving out and if it doesn't match up, we mistake different love for no love. We get lost in translation and find ourselves reeling in pain and disappointment over a massive misunderstanding. It's an endless, unnecessarily complicated cycle. And it needs to break somewhere.

We have to understand that some people are not meant for complex conversations or contemplating the meaning of our existences or nursing all of our wounds back to health. Some people are never going to show up exactly when we need them to, offer us the exact words we need to hear and comfort us in a way that immediately soothes our aching souls. But that doesn't mean that those people are not good and kind and well meaning. It does not mean they don't love us. And, most importantly, it does not mean that they have nothing to offer.

The more we allow ourselves to be disappointed with the people around us, the more we close ourselves off to some of the greatest and most unexpected forms of love. We don't get control over how anyone else manages his or her affection. We don't even get to choose where they allocate it. But here's what we do have control over:

We have control over our reaction to love. We have control over whether or not we recognize that the ride someone gave us to work this morning was love. That the night someone came over and watched a movie with us because they sensed we were upset was love. That the friend who has no idea what advice to offer or what help to give, but who likes our Facebook statuses and invites us over to parties is showing love, in whatever form they know how to show it. We can appreciate those tiny, everyday actions or we can be bitter over them not being enough.

We have control over whether or not we're going to reach

out. We get to choose if we're going to be bitter and isolated or if we're going to take hold of whatever chance we have at connection. If we're going to offer our own love up to others or if we're going to hoard it away and feel confused when others follow our lead. We get to choose if we make the first move when it comes to connection or if we're going to be a further part of the problem. If we're going to be one more person who doesn't show up when they say they will or reach out when others are in need or who wants to receive love first and give it back only when they're sure it's not a risk. We get to decide what kind of love we put out there, even if we cannot control what we get back.

Because at the end of the day, that's the only thing we have control over — how we manage our own care and affection. If you want proof that the kind of love you want to have exists, you're going to have to be the proof. You're going to have to give the kind of love you want to see in the world. You're going to have to be everybody else's reassurance that it exists, that it's all encompassing, that it's there.

The more we pit our hopes and expectations on what others have to offer, the more we facilitate our own heartbreak. But the more we realize what we do have control over, the more we end up growing into bigger, more encompassing versions of ourselves. Versions that never disappoint.

19

Read This If You Feel Like You're Unworthy Of Being Loved

Ari Eastman

Somewhere between the second glass of wine and Netflix obnoxiously asking, "Are you still watching?" a thought crosses your mind that you never wanted to admit. It's an embarrassing sort of darkness you know would just seem like a cry for help. Like some sad Facebook post that we all secretly cringe at.

So you just keep pushing it back down, ignoring this gnawing feeling in the pit of your stomach. You don't want to say it out loud. Because if you say it, maybe you'll give this terrible fear some sort of power. Like you might somehow speak it into truth. And if that happens, what's next?

What's life supposed to look like when you decide love is not something you deserve?

Maybe you know exactly when you first made this toxic self-assessment. You can trace its twisty roots back to childhood, how you watched others on the playground so effortlessly happy and care-free. You wanted to be like them, to fit in without having to overthink every action you made. You craved normalcy. Simplicity. That comforting feeling like you finally belonged.

But you never quite got there.

And so, the idea was planted. Perhaps you won't be like everyone else. Perhaps you don't deserve to be.

Or, maybe even more painful, you have no clue how you came to believe this damaging thought about yourself. It's just always been there — a knowing that you can't shake. You sit and watch everyone around you give and receive. They seem to just understand it. Accept it. Not question why someone could see good in them.

You envy those people. You want to know what happened to fuck you up so eternally. It doesn't seem fair. But you remember, life rarely is. So, you suck it up. You stop asking for answers.

And now here you are, trying to bury this nagging thought that refuses to stay hidden. It's popping up when you least expect it. You're thinking about it when sleep refuses to find you. You're thinking about it in song lyrics, movies, stupid memories that claw at your heart. You can't stop from whispering it when no one else is around to hear. *What if I'm unworthy of love?*

You are. And I understand those two words aren't enough to change how you feel. It's not like a lightbulb just went off and you can finally see a way through this dark path. I get it. I'm not saying anything revolutionary.

You are worthy of love because you've thought about it. You've feared it. You've tossed and turned, trying to figure out how to reach a place of understanding and peace. That means more than you realize.

You're failing to remember how much love *you've* got inside of you. It doesn't always come from an outside source. In fact, we can't rely on external validation. Is it lovely? Of course. But we can't make that our life source.

You might be shaking your head, no way could you ever love yourself. You don't like what you see, who you are, avoid a mirror at all costs. Go ahead! Give me all the excuses in the book. I'm not arguing with you. You probably won't like yourself all the time. Who the hell does??

But whether or not you recognize it, you've got an inner-well of love, and that's the kind of thing that never runs dry. Sometimes, it takes an entire lifetime of searching to realize we had what we needed all along. You are capable of quenching your own thirst.

20

Read This If You're Hopelessly Attracted To The Guy Who Treats You Like Shit

Tatiana Pérez

Emotional fluency is my thing.

Call it a product of my ENFP personality type, or blame my dad, who famously cried at the sight of the sunset on my tenth birthday (it was *just too beautiful*). Or just call it being a woman. Whatever the case, I've never been afraid to express my deepest sentiments. I've never thought my heightened ability to emote was a weakness. I was taught by a highly expressive Latin family to say what I feel without reservation—that's strength, in my world.

Spoiler alert: college guys—American guys in general, really—don't share my temperament. All the young men I've encountered, sexually or otherwise, have been terrified of emotions. I'm being hyperbolic, of course; there've been a select few with an aptitude for emotional articulation. But I'm sure I'm not relaying any particularly novel information when I say that guys avoid feelings at all costs. Feelings aren't manly.

Feelings make you a lil' bitch. The ideal dude, apparently, is something like Patrick Bateman: murderously callous. So heartless and unfeeling that he can divorce all sex—all human interaction—from strong emotions.

And why shouldn't he? Because doesn't our beloved hookup trope revolve around the idea that girls are only interested in guys who treat them like shit? That the moment a dude considers a woman a human being capable of feeling, that woman will immediately lose interest?

I, for one, am horribly guilty of pledging allegiance to that fucked up ideal. To that insidious, gross notion that gentle, genuine displays of affection are somewhat repulsive. I have, on many occasions, rejected a nice guy on the basis of his being nice. Why? Because, for most of my life, I didn't think I deserved a nice guy.

As a kid, I was chubby with a mouthful of metal and rectangular TRANSITION LENS GLASSES (honestly mom, wtf). And hairy. And short. Boys weren't interested. And I thought they never would be. I thought I was ugly. I thought I was totally undesirable (as if a ten year old should feel pressured to be the object of sexual attention).

As a freshman in college, I still thought I was that chubby, short, metal-mouthed, transition-lensed 10 year old. I still thought I was ugly. And undesirable. And undeserving of a guy who would treat me like a person should treat another person. I'm generous—a product of being an older sister I think. And funny. And smart. And attractive. And—when I want to be—kind. I'd joke about how I'd make a great girlfriend, if someone would just give me the chance. And for the first three years of college, no one did. NO ONE—from the senior football captain to the annoying, effeminate nerd—wanted to date me. They all treated me like trash. And I'd keep sleeping with them, because I honestly thought: "Well, better this than nothing."

I was fucked up. I'm still fucked up, but I like to think I've grown a bit since my days of pouring my heart out to mean boys who would shit all over it. I like to think if I were single now, I'd only give myself to a guy as tender and sweet as I hope I've conditioned my little brother to be. My boyfriend's far from a triumph of emotional expression, but he's kind. And usually, he doesn't strive to be an asshole.

There are times, though, when I have to choke his feelings out of him. It can be maddening and no, it's not my responsibility, but I can't help but feel burdened by it. I'm consistently compelled to soften his emotional calluses. To teach him that not every interaction is a business transaction. That emotions aren't necessarily efficient, but that they're always productive. That everybody needs to embrace their doughier inclinations. To say what they feel, and to be better, more whole people for it.

Wish me luck. This shit is exhausting.

21

Read This If Your Friends Are All Moving On Without You

Heidi Priebe

Television lied to us about adulthood.

Most of us grew up watching *Friends, How I Met Your Mother,* or, more recently, *New Girl.* And these shows promised big things for our twenties and thirties. We were supposed to move to a new city, stumble into the closest bar and suddenly find ourselves wrapped up in a group of goofy comrades who would light up our loneliness with their unending charm and devotion.

The characters in those shows stuck together come hell or high water. Sure, sometimes one of them got married or gave birth. But it wasn't a big deal. They'd raised the baby in their rent-controlled Brooklyn flat — right across the hall from their best friends — and conveniently leave it at home anytime the group wanted to go grab coffee together.

And so that's what we figured adulthood would be a like — a series of hapless adventures, strung together through the wisdom and support of our friend group. We were scarcely prepared fro the reality of adulthood — one in which almost everything seems to take priority over our friendships. And we definitely were not prepared for the unfortunate periods of adulthood where our close friends all seemed to be moving on without us — finding bigger and better things while we got left behind in the dust.

It isn't always that way, of course. Sometimes you're the one doing the leaving — and you may not even notice yourself doing so. You accept a job overseas, move in with a significant other, or grow committed enough to your job that you just can't justify nights out with your old group of friends anymore. You quietly and subtly remove yourself from the people who used to matter most to you but it isn't the end of the world — after all, you have bigger fish to fry. You're an adult now. You have real things going on.

But at some point or another, the tables are going to turn — because they always do. You cannot get through adulthood without feeling — at least once or twice — that everyone is moving on without you. It's like skinning your knee or getting detention as a child. It happens to us all and it's just one of those painful, inevitable parts of growing up.

And when it happens, it's rough. One day you're packing four inhabitants into a three person apartment, hosting wild parties, going on hilariously bad dates and reminiscing about it all over takeout dinners on the living room floor. And then in the blink of an eye, it all changes. Someone gets serious with a boyfriend or girlfriend and moves out. Somebody else gets promoted and can now afford a fancy one-bedroom uptown. Someone accepts a job teaching overseas and suddenly you're left all alone, with the same life you've always been living but minus all the characters who once made it so worthwhile.

And when that happens, it's so easy to feel spiteful toward our friends. It's easy to blame them for leaving, for progressing, for getting engaged or promoted or pregnant — even if the 'good' part of us is happy for them throughout it all. It's easy to spend all of our time reminiscing about the way things used to be, and spitefully rejecting the way things are. We don't want new friends, because it won't be the same. We don't want new roommates, because nobody can replace our old ones. We don't want to move forward, because the past looks so much better. The past was a place where there was camaraderie and togetherness and growth. The present is bleak in comparison.

And perhaps here's what we need to remember at those times — that as depressing as the entire experience is, it is a hopelessly normal part of growing up. At some point or another, life tears even the best people apart and it's not always malicious or intentional. It's just the way things happen. There are going to be times in our lives where we want everything to last forever but they simply can't — and it's nobody's fault or responsibility to fix. It's just the way the chips fall. The best times are all fleeting, by their very definition. It's their exceptionality that sets them apart.

So when we arrive at these points in our lives — where the people who've made up all our yesterdays branch off toward their own tomorrows — we have to learn to make peace with their choices. We have to learn to take a step back from resentment and our pride and our loneliness and remember that there are an infinite number of new characters that have yet to make their debut into our lives. That the best times to date are behind us but that doesn't mean the future doesn't hold even better opportunities for friendship and love. But if we remain so fixated on what we've lost, we'll never see what's still left to be found.

Because chances are, there's someone else out there with your exact sense of humour and your same zest for life, feeling hopelessly sad that all their friends have moved on without them. Maybe they're considering putting up an ad for a new roommate, or asking their pretty cool coworker out for a friend-date. Maybe that co-worker's you. Maybe the next person you fall in best-friend love with is a whole lot closer than you'd think.

Or maybe not. Maybe you're still sitting at home sulking over the departure of your close circle and refusing to consider what comes next. Maybe you need to stay there for a while, because you're the kind of person who takes time to mourn what you've lost. But if that's the case, at least keep this in mind: In all of our favorite sitcoms, all our favorite characters had one thing in common — for the most part, they met by random chance. And the more of those chances you take, the better your odds are of finding that next amazing cast.

Because they're out there somewhere — hoping that the next person who stumbles into their favorite bar or coffee shop is someone exactly like you.

22

Read This If You're Struggling To Love Your Body

Tatiana Pérez

"Tati, let me see the dress already!"

I'm 10 years old, and my face is in my hands. I'm sitting in a Bloomingdale's fitting room with a tiny lavender gown around my ankles. It's a size 12 for girls, but it doesn't fit. It never fits.

"No. I hate it."

I swing the door open and leave the soft purple bundle on my mom's lap.

"What was wrong with it? It didn't fit?"

"It fit, ok? But it's ugly and I hate it. Let's go."

I'm not looking at her, but I can feel her sad eyes on my back.

"So let's find another dress, sweetie. I'm sorry you didn't like it."

"Can we just go, please? I don't want to be here anymore."

"Ok, sweetie. Let's go."

My bedroom's next to the kitchen. I wait till I'm sure no one's there. Finally, silence. I hurry to the pantry. Usually, we don't keep sugar in the house. Or any processed snacky shit.

But we had a birthday party for my little brother a few days ago, so the cabinet's brimming with seduction: Oreos, popcorn, pretzels. Even soda in the fridge. I take what I can hold in two arms. Then I lock myself in my room, and I don't come out till dinner.

A few hours is enough to punish myself for the dress. And I feel foul all the while. But I can't stop. Because I opened that fitting room door to a world of self torture. To a world where—when a pillowy child can't fit into the lavender dress the label says *should* fit her—eating always occasions shame. Guilt. Hurt. Hate. So the child sits with her head in her hands and the dress at her ankles and drowns in the tragedy of her soft little body. And then she sneaks away with enemy and eats. And eats. And eats. Always with the intention of starving herself tomorrow.

I used to look at old photos of my mom and hate her while I did. I didn't hate her, of course—but rabid jealousy isn't far off. Because she didn't look like me—from what I can see, all her life, she was narrow and flat. No tits. No ass. And no fat. She was beautiful. Her body was everything mine wasn't, and she didn't have to work for it. She glided through her youth with a perfectly trim figure. She never sat in a fitting room with her head in her hands. Everything fit her. So she ate Oreos and popcorn and pretzels, too, but she never lost herself in them. She never abused food like a heroin addict does dope. She ate when she was hungry, and stopped when she was full. And when she got up from the table, her mind followed. She didn't think about her stomach till it was time for another meal.

But me? I'm not so lucky. Because still today, when I look at my reflection and scorn what I see, all I want is to feed the shame. The guilt. The hurt. The hate. All I want is to eat. And eat. And eat. Always with the intention of starving myself tomorrow.

Two summers ago, my body enmity was at an epic high. And in my experience, there's no sensation quite so mean, quite so insidious, as that of feeling fat in New York City in 90 degree weather. The thick, smoky air settles on your skin like a nylon blanket and your thighs scream as they rub together under your skirt and you look around at all those skinny statues that walk the streets beside you and the self-hate thickens with the smog. And then you lock yourself in your room with whatever you can find: cookies you don't like, dry pasta, days-old rice. And the food's not feeding your hunger; you're not hungry, and you haven't been for an hour. But you can't stop. You'll starve yourself tomorrow.

I remember sitting on the plane to Amsterdam at the end of that long, hot summer and swearing: "This is it, Tati. This is the semester you change your body and you learn to love it. This is the semester you look in the mirror with pride and then you push your plate away when you're finished." And it was. I lost twenty pounds in four months, and I left Europe feeling fucking *incredible*. There were still things I wanted to change about my body, of course. There'll always be things. I could be ten pounds lighter. Ten pounds leaner. Ten pounds harder. But for the first time in a very long time, after that semester, I didn't turn away from my reflection.

The fear is still there. The fear of binging. It's cruel and it hides and it waits for the moments I feel most comfortable in my own skin to overtake my body. And then my insides turn as I stuff them with whatever I can find: cookies I don't like, dry pasta, days-old rice. Always with the intention of starving myself tomorrow. I don't know that the fear will ever leave. That the pattern will ever break. I think it's etched into my bones like the memory of that lavender dress. But I'm getting stronger. And I do love myself. And I do think I'm beautiful.

And dammit, I should be fed.

23

Read This If You're An Empowered Woman Who Has A Lot Of (Bad) Sex

Tatiana Pérez

During freshman orientation, my fellow first years and I were greeted with many a serious conversation about rape and sexual assault. One thing was made painfully clear: Verbal consent from both parties is an *absolute* prerequisite for any sexual interaction.

Our school was magnificently forceful about instilling in us, as a class, a healthy, informed approach to sex. I've always admired that—the administration's unique push to foster an environment of safe sex, where students feel comfortable and overwhelmingly know that, should they be the victim of any non-consensual sex practices, they have countless resources (the deans, counselors at the health center, a 24 hour student-run rape and sexual assault hotline)—to help them find peace and justice.

I applaud my college for its efforts.

What I think was lost on many of us—us as a class, us as a generation, us as a people—however, is that rape and sexual assault, even by their most nuanced legal definitions, are not the sole proponents of unsavory sex. Of bad sex. Of sex that is coercive or abusive in nature, even if it is, technically, consensual.

I've said it once, and I'll say it a million times over: I'm pro slut. I'm all about a woman getting hers as often as she wants, with as many partners as she pleases. I don't believe a woman's virginity is a sacrosanct treasure to be awarded only to the most "deserving," holy man. I don't think we should treat our bodies like accolades—like gifts whose value increases with every minute we "make him wait."

I'm pro slut. I'm pro sexual liberation. I'm furiously pro sex before marriage. I'm pro woman. But I think these declaratives can get tricky. I think, in some terribly treacherous way, knowing and preaching that I'm pro slut, pro sexual liberation, pro sex before marriage, pro woman, even, has, on more than one occasion, helped me rationalize some incredibly unappetizing sex.

I lost my virginity during my freshman year. I lied about not being a virgin to loads of people until that point because I was embarrassed. I didn't want to be a virgin, and I knew that most people who knew me, even if only tangentially, never would've guessed that I still possessed my v-card. And I liked that. But then, freshman year came, and I actually got laid. I've never regretted it—not for a moment. I barely knew the guy but he was hot and into me and the sex wasn't great, but I was psyched when it finally happened.

Not so unexpectedly, the guy who took my virginity turned out to be a consummate asshole. Still, we kept hooking up sporadically throughout my sophomore year. Even a few times when I got back from studying abroad in Amsterdam my junior year. I didn't like him. And the sex was *never* good. But I kept doing it with him—despite his mean demeanor and inability to make me orgasm—because I thought: "I'm 18 to 20. I should be having sex. I *want* to be having sex. I don't want anyone to tell me who I should or shouldn't do it with. I want to do it all the time. That's what being young is all about. That's what being *me* is all about."

Neither he nor any of the other sad boys I slept with during those two years gave an iota of a shit about making me come. None of them were interested in my pleasure. All of them wanted to get in and get out. All of them wanted sex. None of them wanted me.

The story doesn't end all that badly. I found a guy I love as much as I love having sex with him. Every so often, when I think about the two years before him, I cringe. And I feel sorry for myself. I wish I'd been strong enough, then, to wait. To not just fuck for the sake of fucking—for the sake of feeling mature and sexy and, most importantly, empowered.

That's my experience. I certainly can't claim that all (very) sexually active, unattached women share that experience. I don't actually think they do. I'm sure plenty of young women have a lot of good sex with a lot of partners. But I think there are a lot of empowered, feminist young women who share my plight, too.

So to those women, all I ask is that you love your body, and that you appreciate yourself. And that every time you have sex, you have sex for *you*. Not for some nebulous ideal. Not for the fuck of it. Not for him.

24

Read This If You Feel Like It's Taking You Too Long To Move On

Heidi Priebe

Everybody seems to have a different rule about how long it should take you to get over something. If it's a relationship, they tell you half the length of it. If it's a loss they tell you approximately a year — long enough to go through each special occasion when you're used to having them by your side. We use language like 'moving on' and 'letting go' as though they're actions as simple as shutting a door and physically walking away. We uncurl our fingers and drop whatever we are holding — that's letting go, right? That's all it takes?

I don't think I've experienced a single loss in my life that I've gotten over in the time frame that seems to have been allotted by society as 'acceptable.' And I suspect that I'm not alone there. It is not human nature to let go. We are, at our core, territorial creatures. We fight to hold onto what we love. Giving up isn't in any way instinctual.

If there's anything I wish we could talk more about it's the in-between stages of letting someone go. Because nobody lets go in an instant. You let go once. And then you let go again.

And then again and again and again. You let someone go at the grocery store when their favorite type of soup is on sale and you don't buy it. You let them go again when you're cleaning your bathroom and have to throw out the bottle of the body wash that smells like them. You let them go that night at the bar when you go home with somebody else or you let them go every year on the anniversary of the day you lost them. Sometimes you're going to have to let one person go a thousand different times, a thousand different ways, and there's nothing pathetic or abnormal about that. You are human. And it isn't always as simple as making one decision and never looking back.

Moving on isn't always about speeding enthusiastically forward so much as it's about having one foot on the gas and the other on the brakes — releasing and accelerating in turn. You're not a failure for getting to someplace amazing and still feeling like a part of yourself is missing once you get there. You're not pathetic for mourning while you grow. The bad things don't disappear in the blink of an eye and the good things don't spring up into existence without reigning at least a tiny bit of collateral damage. It takes time for everything to even out. And it should.

The truth is, none of us want to think of ourselves as works in progress. We want everything to happen instantaneously: Falling in love, falling out of it, letting go of what we know we ought to leave in the past and moving on to whatever comes next. We hate the in-between spaces — the times when we're okay but not quite there yet. The periods where we suspect that growth is happening but have nothing to show for it. The days when everything feels like it's falling into place and yet we still go home and cry into our pillow because there's nobody to share our good fortune with. If success is a staircase, we are eternally taking two steps forward and one step back and that's okay. That's how we keep ourselves in check. It's how we keep ourselves from blowing the whole she-bang.

We have to be patient with ourselves as we move through the parts in between the where we've been and where we're going. We have to let the chasm motivate rather than dishearten us. It's okay to not be there yet. It's okay to be unsure of every step that you take forward. We don't talk about how moving on sometimes feels like we're fighting every part of our most basic instincts, but we should. We should talk about how growth is often every bit as painful as it is beautiful.

Because growth and letting go are so complexly intertwined that we often only see one or the other. We forget that they can exist side by side — releasing the old while letting in the new. We forget that we have the ability to do the exact same thing. And that if we'd only stop beating ourselves up over it, we might realize just how far we've already come.

25

Read This If There's Something You Can't Forgive Yourself For

Heidi Priebe

We all like to separate ourselves neatly into virtues and vices.

We like think of our depravities as independent agents — acting out of character and rallying against our better judgment. When we fail, we point fingers at our vices. When we hurt someone, we claim we're going to change.

We enjoy creating internal these internal dichotomies because they give us someone to blame when we mess up. Our truest selves are our good selves, our moral selves, the third-party versions of ourselves who recognize that what we did was wrong. We criticize the lesser parts of ourselves for indulging our vices and letting our virtues lay dormant. We tell ourselves we should have known better.

None of us want to admit that there are times in our lives where our virtues and our vices are entirely indistinguishable from one another — but the uncomfortable truth is, there are. The same hunger, curiosity and enthusiasm that spurs all of our greatest accomplishments also propels us toward our greatest mistakes. The same love and compassion that makes us the brightest, most giving versions of ourselves also makes us into the most wretched and unforgivable versions. We cannot ever cut the evil cleanly from ourselves. It's woven through everything we do.

And perhaps it is these morally ambiguous situations that we find it the most difficult to forgive ourselves for. When we can't separate our good parts from our evil parts, we become paralyzed with indecision. We think that we're helping the people around us by holding our volatile inner selves hostage but the truth is, it's a self-interested move. We don't want to come to terms with what we've done and so stay angry at ourselves as a means of disconnecting from it. *I didn't do that*, we tell ourselves, *some horrible, warped version of me did*. We feel angry at that part of ourselves, in an oddly disconnected fashion. We let ourselves believe that we can so neatly detach from who we've been. Except we can't. And here's the uncomfortable truth:

You did something shitty. Something wrong. Something that every pure, well-meaning part of you wishes you could take back and make right.

Except you can't. Sometimes in life, there are no second chances.

And that's okay. It's okay because it has to be.

The truth of the matter is, whether you're a good person or a bad person is simply a story that you tell yourself.

You are no longer the person who did the horrible things that you did in your past — the mere fact that you are holding yourself accountable is a clear indication of that. But what you are now is afraid — that the person who emerged in you before can and is going to reemerge again. That they will compel you again. Take you over again. Wreak chaos on your life and your choices like they did once before.

And that is the story that you have to stop telling yourself — because that story is a self-fulfilling prophecy. That story is the muck on your shoes that you will drag through the homes of everyone you love until the day that you decide to get clean. By refusing to forgive yourself, you are telling yourself a story about shame and obliteration — so many times that it becomes the only one you know how to act out. It becomes the story that you bring into the future, rather than the one you lay peacefully to rest where it belongs.

The real reason you have to choose forgiveness is because it's only the selfless thing left to do. Because by hiding from all of your darkness, you're denying the world of your light. Of your virtue. Of the parts of yourself that are capable of coming back to life to restore the joy and the hope that is needed in the wake of your greatest mistakes.

When you let yourself accept all of those evil, unfathomable parts of yourself you simultaneously offer yourself the chance to evolve beyond them. To grow past them. To accept that you may never be the endlessly virtuous person you once considered yourself to be, but with the death of that idealistic self comes the birth of a realer, more capable one.

One who knows the their capacity for both light and darkness.

And who nonetheless chooses the light.

26

Read This If You Never Know How To Say Goodbye

Heidi Priebe

When you don't know how to the big goodbyes, you live them.

You come home an hour early from work to make extra time. You leave homemade cookies lying on the counter. You make a series of tiny allowances that you wouldn't usually make because you know that the clock is winding down and your time is running short and you suddenly need to make the most of it. You're suddenly aware of how little time you harness for love.

When you do not know how to say goodbye, you extrapolate it. You say goodbye by focusing a little bit harder and listening a little more intently and laughing a little bit louder at what your loved ones say. You part ways by saying 'Yes' when you'd normally tell someone 'No' and you allow yourself to absorb the people and experiences and chances that you'd usually let pass you by. You say goodbye by carving out time for the life you should have always been living. You say goodbye by delving deeper in.

When you do not know how to say goodbye, you feel it.

You feel it in the pit of your stomach when you close the front door of someone's apartment or speed away from a city on a train or print your boarding pass to somewhere far-away at the airport. You feel the full weight of unspoken goodbyes like a mysterious absence inside of you; emptiness that theorizes fullness. Bleakness that balances a whole world full of color.

Because the truth is, we don't ever need to say goodbye to each other. We don't need to clasp hands and kiss cheeks and drive one another to the airport just to put off the inevitable farewell. We just need to remember to live together while we've still got the chance.

We need to keep track of our time as it's running closer and closer to empty. We need to remember to open our hearts and our minds and our thoughts and our lives up to each other, while we still have the time left to connect.

We need to stay up too late and put in too much effort and be bold enough to take all of the chances that we're terrified to take on each other. We have to remember to live every day as if the next will be our greatest goodbye, because this is the greatest gift that we can give one another. The strength to live with a wide-open heart.

Because the truth about our greatest and most genuine goodbyes is that they are truly more like hellos.

More like, *Hello. Our time is winding down and so I'm finally ready to appreciate you fully.*

More like, *Hello. You've been here all this time and I've been blind. Why don't we use this time to carve out what we can.*

More like, *Hello. This is what I've always wanted to tell you. This is my bravery, raging because I am going away. This is who I wish I'd had the courage to be all along.*

Because there's one simple thing we're trying to convey to every person we choose to say goodbye to, it is the simple message that *you mattered.*

It is the expression that *life wouldn't be the same without you — even if your impact was so fleeting or so short that we leave the word 'goodbye' left unsaid.*

But you mattered and I will not forget you. You mattered, so I have to find a way to tell you goodbye, even if I cannot say it outright.

And so, if you don't know how to say goodbye, you live it. You take every last chance you've got. You show up for people. You let them affect you one last time.

You open your world in all the ways that you've been holding back from doing for so long. You let the avoidance of saying goodbye swell and bolster and break open your heart one last time. And then you do the final brave thing, and you leave.

27

Read This If You Feel Like You're Going To Be Single Forever

Johanna Mort

Most days, I don't mind being single. It's pretty great actually. There's a wonderful freedom that comes from being completely and utterly unattached. However, some days, I do mind. It gets lonely. And today is one of those days, so I'm going to talk about it.

*Here's a cue for those who are going to say that I need to stop 'complaining' and do something if singlehood bothers me so much — go ahead and make your comment and move on with your day.

Finding a partner and building a life is such a staple expectation that everyone has about growing old, and I think that's why we can feel so empty when we don't have that. We're conditioned to believe that everything else in life is secondary. Building a career, having hobbies, finding fulfillment. All of it comes after getting married and having kids. And maybe that's how it should be. I don't know. What I *do* know is that that puts a hell of a lot of pressure on dating. And that's terrifying for people like me who just cannot, for whatever reason, get a handle on this whole dating thing.

A summary of my romantic history:

> **10-years-old:** A boy LIKE-liked me for two months. He was popular (on the basketball team *swoon*). For about a week, classmates in my reading class hotly debated whether or not he was going to hold my hand in between social studies and band. (Spoiler alert: he didn't.)

> **21-years-old:** A very drunk man invited me to a birthday party he was having the following day. He called me beautiful. That was both the first and last time that ever happened to me.

Are we all caught up? Fantastic.

The way I see it, there are two possible reasons as to why I'm single and always have been.

Option 1:

I'm a hideous troll monster and the very sight of me physically repulses men.

Option 2:

My personality is capital T, capital W The Worst and men cannot stand to be in my presence for longer than 5 minutes before they want to gouge their eardrums out with a dull spork.

Of the two options, I would much prefer that I'm single because I'm a hideous troll monster. I can change that. I can go jogging (*weeps into the void at the thought*), forgo brownies and ravioli (*screams in vain as all sound is carried away by the wind*), and actually attempt to master the art of make-up (*shrugs, yeah that's do-able*).

But why? Let's say that I get in shape and wear make-up, and I'm swarmed by all those mythical male beings that I've heard might actually exist. Am I to live in fear that the moment I gain a few pounds or lay off the make-up routine that I'll suddenly become unlovable again?

I never like to explore the second option. That it's just me. People don't like *me*.

There's a unique kind of blow that your confidence takes when you've been virtually invisible to the opposite sex for your entire life. When the bouncer at the bar grins and tells your friend that her ID photo doesn't do her justice and then barely gives you a first glance as he waves you through a moment later. When guys come to you for advice on how to ask out your friend. When the only people that ask for your phone number are CVS cashiers trying to apply your membership discount. (On the bright side, I'm fairly certain that I could commit any crime and get away with it.)

As each year passes and nothing changes, you get more and more used to it. You joke about getting cats and saving tons of money on Valentines and anniversary presents, while simultaneously grieving. Grieving because you didn't get that young love. There weren't any sleepless nights spent texting that person that gave you butterflies with each letter sent. You didn't get to sneak out of your parents' house and meet them in "your spot." You didn't get to hold someone's hand for the first time and be the first person to hold their hand, and feel excitement and terror bubble up in your stomach from being in such uncharted territory.

You didn't get any of that and now you're at an age where hooking up is commonplace and you're still hoping that maybe someone wants to hold your hand sometime.

You feel as if Life has moved on without you and as more and more time passes you have less and less of an idea of where you're even supposed to start.

On the best days, it's a nagging worry in the back of your mind, like that squash in your fridge that you keep forgetting to cook. On the worst days, it's overwhelming.

You get to the point where all those milestones that other people look fondly back upon are burdens for you. You have to either bury the idea that your first kiss will be "special" and just "get it over with" so you're a little less different than all your friends, or you can keep holding out hope that someday someone will come around and they'll be okay with taking everything as fast or as slow as you need.

And maybe I'm just stubborn. Maybe I'm making everything much more complicated than it needs to be. That's very possible. I've had ample time to over think absolutely everything.

I don't want some fairy tale, but I want someone to like me for who I am. I'm not going to change myself to fit some mold that feels inauthentic and foreign and leaves a shell of a person that even I cannot recognize in the mirror. This is who I am. Hideous troll monster warts and all. If that means I'll be on my own until my cats and I revert to star dust, then so be it. I am who I am, and most days that's enough.

28

Read This If You Have Embarrassed Yourself Recently

Heidi Priebe

There is a specific, gut wrenching feeling that comes along with remembering an embarrassing experience. And it's one that none of us are exempt from.

You're out walking around in the world when suddenly that mortifying experience from two weeks ago pops into your mind — and instantly all you want is for the sidewalk to split in half and swallow you whole so you can disappear below it and never be seen again. You are immediately certain that every person who has ever seen you embarrass yourself is thinking about you in that exact moment — reliving what you've done in excruciating detail and judging you without remorse. That the people on the street around you, even, can sense something is off — that you have done something deeply shameful and they can see through your flimsy act.

In reality, we remember our own embarrassments with a frequency and amplitude that is absolutely impossible to replicate. Those who witness our embarrassments rarely think any more of it after they've had a quick chuckle at our expense, or experienced a twinge of empathy for us. They certainly are not walking around weeks later reliving our embarrassing moment in their minds. They are consumed by their own concerns, their own commitments and their own past embarrassments. They scarcely have the time or energy to focus on ours.

But that doesn't stop us from reliving our own. Embarrassment has the unique ability to stop us dead in our tracks and make us genuinely consider changing our names, packing a bag for Alaska and never coming home. It makes us yearn for a memory-erasing serum that we can apply to every person who remembers something shameful we have done. We want our embarrassments to be a world away from us but instead we have to live right inside of them, under the pitiful roof that shame built.

None of us can escape embarrassment in our lives — but what we scarcely consider is the idea that it can be a wholly productive experience. Because here's the thing about embarrassment — it is born, almost exclusively, from trying too hard. It's the absolute opposite of apathy. It shows that we went too far, pushed too hard, put ourselves a little too out there and didn't have it work out as planned. Embarrassment is an undesirable sentiment but it's also a noble one in its own right. It declares, by definition, "I did not sit back and let the world happen to me." It's a product of taking life assuredly by the reigns, even if you did not end up where you meant to go.

It is my formal opinion that a well-lived life would be chock full of tiny embarrassments. Moments where you put your heart and your thoughts and yourself on the line and had them rejected. Times when you drank too much or laughed too loudly or loved too fiercely for other people to understand. Times when you were too much yourself for the world to make sense of. Times when your blood was pumping loudly and quickly enough to let you know, without a doubt, that you were more alive in that moment than some people ever get to be in their lifetimes.

Embarrassment is a product of something gone wrong in the short-term, but something gone right in the bigger scheme. It's a product of being the kind of person who tries too hard, lives too fully, gives themselves too completely to every task that they undertake. It's the product of being someone who goes unashamedly for what they want instead of sitting on the sidelines wondering what it would be like to have actually tried.

So much of what we want in life lies on the other side of embarrassment. We want to ask out that person but we don't want them to reject us. We want to apply for that promotion but we don't want our colleagues to know we didn't get it. We want to enjoy our lives as fully and completely as possible but we don't want to be slapped with the loathsome burden of not fitting in. We want everything to come to us effortlessly and shamelessly, without taking any risks. We forget that life doesn't work that way. We forget that embarrassment naturally shows up along the path to pursuing any sort of life that actually matters.

Embarrassment is the pesky side effect of the miracle drug that is courage. We don't want to be humiliated and we don't want to feel ashamed but we do want the biggest, best lives that are possible for ourselves. And embarrassment is a necessary byproduct of that. It's the reminder that we're taking more risks than we're ready for. That we're putting ourselves out there in ways we aren't quite comfortable with. That we're stretching ourselves beyond our own comfort zones and that it's working. Embarrassment is a necessary component of a life that's being lived fully and intensively.

So if you've wanted the sidewalk to swallow you whole over the past week or two, congratulations. You're feeling that way because you've done something brave. Because you've put yourself out on the line. Because you've tried for something and come up short, but at least you tried at all. You're embarrassed because you went for it. And counter-intuitive as it may seem, that feeling of embarrassment almost always means that you are on the right track. You just have to keep moving on past it — after all, all the best stuff is on the other side.

29

Read This If You're Dating A Workaholic And It (Kind Of) Sucks

Tatiana Pérez

We knew it would be tough. I knew it would be tough—he warned me, and I knew. We're a month in, and whaddaya know, we were right—it's tough.

I hauled my ass down on an over-crowded, under-ventilated Peter Pan bus to visit him for the long weekend—five unpleasant hours from Williamstown to Port Authority. I told my parents I was coming home to visit them, too—I think they know that if it weren't for him, I would've stayed at school to study for midterms. But this was supposed to be his first work-free weekend since he started his job, so exams be damned: I was getting on that bus, no matter how sharply that coach stunk of urine.

When I got here, though, I was slapped with a sad reality check; in his line of work, when you're his kind of guy, oftentimes, the job steals what little freedom it promised you—he'd been staffed, and he'd have to put in plenty of weekend hours, after all. So here I am, sitting on my parents' couch, writing a story I didn't think I'd write today, while he grinds. He's not sure when he'll be done—certainly not in time for dinner, but hopefully before 10 p.m. Today is Saturday, btw.

We knew it would be tough. I knew it would be tough—he warned me, and I knew. We're a month in, and whaddaya know, we were right—it's tough.

I was, admittedly, mildly heartbroken when he delivered the shitty news. He works ungodly hours while I attend a maximum 150 minutes of class per day and regularly wake up after 11 a.m.—our schedules are completely out of sync, and even though we "talk" everyday, it's just that: "talk." A "hi" from him during his coffee break. An immediate "hey what's up!" from me. Silence for a few hours. Another "hi" at dinner—his texts are signals of life more than they are conversation-starters. And I don't blame him—he's just started a career that'll exhaust his humanity for the first few years, and then probably still; I don't expect him to set aside his work to exchange sweet nothings with me during his 18-hour day. I never did.

Inevitably, though, disappointment consumes; when he told me our weekend together was no more, my initial thought was not, "That's totally ok, babe, I understand." It was, irrationally, "Um.....fuck you, fuck your job, fuck this. I'm gonna go cry into a fat tub of Nutella and plot the ruin of American capitalism, now."

We knew it would be tough. I knew it would be tough—he warned me, and I knew. We're a month in, and whaddaya know, we were right—it's tough.

Here's the great paradox of this shitty ordeal: Acute workaholism inconveniences our relationship in a million ways, but the symptoms—ambition, energy, diligence, confidence—are among the many reasons why I love him. He's a smart, driven, self-motivated dude; he knows what he wants, and he's happy to sweat through his twenties to get it.

And I *love* that about him.

And I'm proud of him—if I were to disclose his job, you'd be impressed. Everyone's impressed. He's the clean-shaven, tireless kid most parents wish they had. And he *loves* his work, too—that's the best part. He really, really loves it. And he rarely—and I mean *rarely*—complains about the price. So, ultimately, *I* love his work, too. Because I love him, and he loves it—and he wouldn't be the same guy if he didn't.

We knew it would be tough. I knew it would be tough—he warned me, and I knew. We're a month in, and whaddaya know, we were right—it's tough.

But then, no one ever told me relationships were easy.

30

Read This If You're Feeling Betrayed By Your Boyfriend Or Girlfriend

Mélanie Berliet

As you grow closer as a couple, your wellbeing depends increasingly upon the choices your partner makes, both good and bad, in addition to those you make as an individual. When you navigate the world from within the context of a relationship, you're no longer alone in the cockpit, steering your own destiny—a phenomenon that's wonderfully rewarding when things go smoothly, but terribly heart wrenching when things go poorly.

Depending on the parameters of your relationship, messing up can mean a lot of different things. Every couple lives by the rules of their own unwritten (but hopefully well understood) contract. Whatever the terms, however, each person is destined to step outside the bounds of what's considered appropriate conduct on occasion. We're all fallible, after all.

Betrayals of varying degrees of significance are inevitable in a long-term relationship. If you dare to love passionately, missteps are part of the bargain. You are likely to betray—and to feel betrayed by—the person you care about most sometimes.

And when this happens—when one person in a relationship fucks up royally—the fallout undoubtedly sucks for both parties. For the person who made a mistake, it sucks to feel the pangs of guilt specific to hurting someone you adore more than anyone else in the world. For the wronged party, it sucks to feel the ache of a wound so deep and painful, only someone you love madly could have cut it.

The thing is, what happens in the aftermath of a betrayal often matters more than the betrayal itself. The injured party must make a choice: They can remain bitter, or they can forgive, and move forward.

It's tempting to indulge vengeful fantasies. The desire to exact revenge—to inflict pain of equal measure on the person who elicited it in you—is entirely natural. It seems just, especially if you're in the midst of nursing an open wound. An eye for an eye, right? Wrong.

Revenge will *not* taste sweet if it means hurting your significant other—at least, it won't as long as you still genuinely love them. So if you want to salvage your bond, don't reduce yourself to your partner's level. Mimicking their misdeeds will only prolong the hurt on both ends. Other people's lapses in judgment aren't a license to act stupid or to make bad decisions. It isn't fair to invoke suffering simply because you yourself are suffering. Hurting someone deliberately is a grave crime, especially in the name of payback.

Healthy romantic relationships aren't built on tit-for-tat. They're built on the courage to admit wrongdoing, and the strength to pardon one another. Behaving like a kind, respectable adult is never ill advised, no matter your partner's infraction. Set the standard. Be a good person first, and a loving boyfriend or girlfriend second. Forgive. Say "I forgive you!" out loud, when no one's around. Then say it to your significant other's face. Forgiveness is about so much more than absolving someone. It's the antidote to internal suffering, also. Those three powerful words will free you from the burden of pain, resentment, and overthinking—as long as you actually mean them.

Don't forgive anyone if you don't mean it, but don't wallow in bitterness if you don't have to, either. Forgiveness isn't easy, of course. It demands fortitude and resolve. But if you can find it in yourself to choose forgiveness, it always proves worthwhile. Embrace it as wholeheartedly and quickly as humanly possible. If you can't get there, consider ending the relationship before your spite burns it alive.

31

Read This If You Grew Up Always Wanting To Be Older

Heidi Priebe

I, like many others, have spent my entire life wanting to be older.

I hated being a kid. I craved independence from the day that I took my first step. I sought for freedom from the moment I took my first breath. I always wanted to have more choice, more independence, more opportunity, even more responsibility than I was awarded at such a young age. The joy of childhood was in some ways lost on me because I simply wanted to get it all over with and grow up.

When I finally reached adulthood, it did not disappoint. The day I turned eighteen was perhaps the best day of my life. I was finally considered independent in the eyes of the law and I wanted to take full advantage: to rush into adult jobs and grown-up apartments and serious relationships. My quest to be older didn't stop after childhood and to be honest, I'm not sure if it ever will. I always have my eye on what's coming five, ten, twenty years down the line. I am future oriented and that's an asset in so many ways. But it can be also disadvantageous.

The problem with obsessing over the future is that we never really get there. We turn twenty-five and start planning for the year we turn thirty. We get the job of our dreams and immediately fixate on that next promotion. We live eternally in the future and never in the now. And that's not necessarily a bad thing – until occasionally when the present catches up and forces us to realize that we're not living ten or twenty years in the future. We're living now. And every now and then we get blind sighted by desires that are entirely typical for the age we're at.

This is a friendly reminder for all future-oriented individuals that it's okay to simply be the age you are.

When you're young and you're free, you don't have to have it all figured out. You're allowed to be a little unsure. You're allowed to be a little bit lost. You're allowed to work a job that isn't your dream job or date someone you're not sure you could marry or waste time at a hobby you enjoy that isn't necessarily taking you anywhere career-wise. Not everything has to have a clear, long-term purpose. You're allowed, in some ways, to simply be the age you are. To enjoy the ride. To figure it out as you go.

You're allowed to date without worrying too hard about where it's going — to enjoy someone for their presence and not their future husband or wife potential. You're allowed to kiss a few strangers and have a few flings and go out with someone for the sole reason of they make you laugh and you kind of want to see them without clothes on. You don't have to think so hard about all of it. Some things are allowed to be instinctual.

You're allowed to not date at all. You're allowed to enjoy

time on your own and plan your life alone and change those plans when and if it becomes necessary. You don't have to grow preoccupied over your compatibility with others or what that date with that guy from last weekend really meant — you're allowed to simply let people come and go as it makes sense. You don't have to be putting yourself out there when you're not really feeling like doing so. It's okay to be alone if that is what you want. It doesn't mean you'll end up that way indefinitely.

You're allowed to get out of your comfort zone. You're allowed to strap on a backpack and go traveling while everyone else is getting married and promoted and popping out babies. You're allowed to take that job that you aren't sure about because it might be a good opportunity, even if you have to move across the country to take it. You're allowed to jump feet-first into things that are a little uncertain. You are young enough to bounce back if it doesn't work out. You are old enough to deal with the fallout of your misjudgments.

You don't have to live your life based on a careful, outdated timeline that you set up for yourself when you were too young to ever know better. You may not be where you thought you'd be at twenty-five or thirty-five or fifty but maybe you're altogether better because of it. After all, the best parts of life are the unplanned bits — the people or the projects or the passion that interrupt your plans without apology and take your life by storm.

Because that's the irony of growing up — maturity is not derived from following a pre-decided timeline with precision. The moments that truly test and challenge us are the unexpected ones — the ones that force us to stretch and alter ourselves in ways that we truly did not plan for. These are the moments that grow us the most. They are the times that reveal our true character.

The irony of growing up is that in order to do so authentically, we have to stop trying so hard. Experience comes to us most fully in the moments that we do not expect and that we deal with entirely greenly. We fumble our way through so many of life's pivotal moments and, frankly, we ought to. We cannot plan ahead for the things that truly matter. We cannot map out the moments that will change us because those do not happen in the future. They happen in real time, in our actual, tangible lives. And they alter the future correspondingly.

The moments that truly grow us up are the ones that happen when we're least expecting them. And the final irony is that they are so often the moments that make us feel intensely, insurmountably young.

32

Read This If You're Keeping A Secret That You're Ashamed Of

Heidi Priebe

If there's anything I've learned from writing extensively online it's this: None of our experiences are entirely unique.

We're all fighting our own battles, and no two are the same — that much is true. We're all facing down personal demons, struggling to conquer our psyches and trying to become better people. We're all afraid to share what's going wrong. And yet, there isn't a single personal article I've ever shared that hasn't been met with at least one email lamenting, "I'm going through the exact same thing and I thought that I was the only one."

Many of those messages come through Facebook. Most of them come attached to a shiny, polished photo of a person who seems to be radiating joy. They're on a beach in Mexico holding a Mojito. They're at home holding a young, happy child. They're in a wedding dress kissing their partner or they're in running shoes, finishing a marathon. They're the last people you'd expect to be scared, reeling or lost. And yet they're there in abundance — claiming their deep insecurities and expressing utter relief over learning that they're not alone.

Here's the truth about how we're all doing, as far as I understand it:

We all feel like we're pretending more often than not. None of us are sure that we've got it together. We're all a little bit lost, a little bit inadequate, a little bit broken and a little exposed. We're all disenchanted with some portion of where we've been. We're all scared shitless of what comes next.

We've all been hopelessly in love with someone who doesn't love us back and heartbroken over someone who we thought we could trust. We've all lost ourselves a little inside of a relationship that consumed us too fully. We've all traversed through the dark, barren wasteland of heartbreak. We've all felt betrayed and blind sighted and broken, and we all blame ourselves for it in some way. We've all, in some measure, been dishonest in love ourselves.

We all think that we're horrible people, deep down. We've all done things that have forced a pit of shame to pool in the bottom of our stomachs and for most of us, that shame has been festering for a long, long time. We're all worried that someone we love is going to discover our dark parts and then cease to love us. We're all desperate to cover our tracks. We'll all do almost anything to hide the parts of ourselves that we think are impure and unlovable.

If there's anything I wish we all understood a little more fully, it's this: We are never, ever, ever alone.

You're not the only person with a broken family, a broken spirit or a broken soul. You're not the only one who's scared of things that other people don't seem to be scared of and can't figure out why. You're not the only person who's depressed or anxious or compulsive in ways that make no sense to you. You're not the only person who's scared to ask for help. We are all a little broken. We're all insecure. And at some point, every single one of us is incapable of handling it all on our own.

You're not the only person who's been lied to or cheated on or abused. You're not the only person who didn't know how to defend themselves when they needed to most. You're not the only one who's still hurting from a wound that was inflicted on them long, long ago. You're not the only one who thinks that they're taking too long to heal. You may be lost and confused and desperate but if there's one thing you are not, it's alone in it. We're a collection, a society, a nation full of broken hearts and fractured parts. And yet, we are all still here. We're all still struggling through every day. And we all somehow think that we're the only ones suffering.

We beat ourselves up over the secrets we keep. We hold ourselves back through them. We loathe and hate and scathe ourselves for what we haven't done yet, what we should have figured out by now, where we haven't gotten to in life and where everyone else around us has. We forget that we're not the only ones keeping secrets. That we're not the only ones harboring shame. That if we're liars, cheaters and fakes, so is everyone else that surrounds us.

We forget that it's okay to be a little bit broken. It's okay to be shameful and fractured. That it's okay to not have it all figured out. We forget because nobody tells us. Because we collectively choose to put a brave face on and push those secrets down.

And perhaps there is no easy answer to any of it. There's

no quick fix, no life hack, no single way to pick our fractured hearts up off the floor and piece them back together. But what we can do is show a little more patience for ourselves in the process of doing so — a little more care, a little more under-standing and a little less disgust.

We're all harbouring shame. We're all holding onto secrets. But we're all still here, simply doing the best we can.

And no matter how much it feels like it, we're never, ever alone.

33

If You're Unsure Whether Or Not You Can Trust Them, Read This

Heidi Priebe

We're an incredibly infidelious nation.

I wish this weren't the uncomfortable truth, but it is. We cheat on each other. We lie to each other. We have endless options available to us these days, literally at the tip of our fingers — a simple "Swipe left" or "Swipe right" gets us what we crave almost effortlessly. We have infinite possibilities available to us and yet we still crave companionship. We want love. We want togetherness. We want trust, but it's getting harder and harder to come by.

Trust doesn't come easy anymore. Especially not to those who've been cheated on, lied to or maltreated in the past. Each new relationship presents a challenge: Do you trust them or do you shy away? Do you guard yourself or do you give in? Do you invest your full heart or do you tread as lightly as possible — easing into every relationship with minimum investment until you are as certain as you can be that they're not going to let you down?

The risk of letting our guard down seems insurmountable

at times. We work hard to build up lives that we're proud of: jobs we're happy with, homes we cherish, friends and families who surround us with love. The possibility of inviting another person in to share in all of that, without the guarantee that it's going to work out, can be paralyzing. How do we know they won't turn on us? How do we know it'll work out?

And the truth is, we don't. Whether or not we can trust someone will always be a tough bet to wager. But it's also a futile guessing game. And it's one that can destroy your entire relationship before it even begins.

The truth is, we're all capable of infidelity. We're all capable of monogamy. There is no genetic code, no telltale sign, no one situation that guarantees infidelity or faithfulness. There are influencing factors, of course. There are predispositions based on gender or personality, arguably. But there is no certain way to predict whether or not the person you're about to fall head over heels for is going to be faithful to you. There just isn't. That's the truth.

And so where does that leave us? We can calculate our odds straight to hell and back — listing positive traits on one hand and suspicious behaviors on another. We can sneak peeks at their cell phone, do investigative work on their track history and slip subtle questions into conversation. All ideal first and second date activities. But at the end of the day, we'll never find the answers we're searching for. We'll never be capable of predicting the future. Getting lied to, being betrayed, getting cheated on are always going to be risks we are taking when we enter into a new relationship.

We don't always get the answers that we want about the future but if we're living our lives right we don't need them.

Because at the end of the day, trust has nothing to do with the person you're dating. It isn't a magical feeling that springs into existence when someone passes our theoretical tests and says all the right things at all the right times. Trust is a decision. Trust is the waking, conscious choice to invest in another human being because you know that even if they betray you, you'll be okay.

Whether or not we can trust someone always comes back to how we feel about ourselves — it's a reflection of what we feel capable of dealing with. Trust doesn't mean, "I know you'll never hurt me." It means, "I trust myself to deal with the fallout if you do."

Trying to predict the future is maddening at best and relationship-destroying at worst. Any potential relationship runs the risk of failing. Of collapsing. Of leaving us high and dry after we invested ourselves in someone who stopped choosing us back. But when it comes to trust, here are the only questions you really need to ask:

Can you trust yourself? If it all goes to hell, can you pick yourself up off the floor and start again? Are you strong enough? Are you capable of dealing with the fallout?

If the answer is no, now might not be the best time to consider a relationship.

And if the answer is yes, you have nothing to worry about at all.

34

Read This If You've Ever Lived In A Small Town

Marisa Donnelly

The jingle of the gas station bell. The hum of the coffee machine. The donuts made fresh every morning. And the man behind the counter who knows your order before you ask, who hands you your coffee, extra cream, and says, "This one's on me."

The mother in her dented red mini-van who waves from the same intersection, James and 3rd, every school day morning.

The lady in her electric wheelchair with the dog leash wrapped around the controller, taking Pepper for his morning walk. Who asks you how your day is, if you're happy, if you're dating anyone.

The trees that outline the park, branches swaying in the wind. The little flowers that line the concrete road right outside of the elementary school.

These are the things you will see in a small town.

The woman jogging the block who smiles as she runs past you. The teenager that nods his head as you let him cross at the stop sign.

The cows that line the fields just off Highway 9. The unlit

backroads that are so dark at night, if you turn off your lights, you disappear. The gravel paths that you travel and intentionally lose yourself along.

The faces that see you, smile at you. That seem to recognize you, know you, care about you.

That is what you will see in a small town.

A small town is three restaurants, two gas stations, and a bar that feels like a second home. It is a man sharing a morning beer and breakfast with another man, fresh from the night shift.

It is a single mother with three daughters in daycare. It is a teenage boy on the edge of his seat, itching to run.

It is worn steps, laundry on a clothesline, children playing in the back alley, and tired, happy faces.

It is cheaper gas, friend discounts, and never having your I.D. on you because everyone knows who you are.

A small town is hugs shared between acquaintances. Friendship despite an age gap, 20-somethings and 65-year-olds, teenagers and 10-year-olds. Somebody's related to somebody. Someone knows someone who knows so-and-so. It is strangers that are family.

If you've ever lived in a small town, you know this: You can hide, but you are never invisible. You can be alone, but never lonely. You have an urge to leave, but there's an even stronger pull luring you back. You love and are loved.

That is what it means to live in a small town.

35

Read This If You Are Still In The Closet And Struggling To Come Out

Jacob Geers

October 11th is National Coming Out Day, and I wanted to write some cute list article to commemorate it. I was thinking something along the lines of "27 Things All LGBT Who Have Come Out Understand" or "18 Different Things Everyone Who Has Come Out Has Experienced." I toyed with the article for days, and became frustrated with how little progress I was making.

Then it struck me, the truth so close and plain it could have been hitting on me at a club. I wasn't getting anywhere with the article because there probably are no 27, 18, or even 3 things that universally unite everyone who has had to come out about a sexual orientation or gender identity, and if there are, I certainly don't know them.

> *It's okay. It may not seem like it right now, but you are going to be fine. I know it's scary, but don't be afraid. You are who you are, and you should love that person, and I don't want anyone to have to go*

through 22 years of their life afraid to accept that.
– Connor Franta

The truth is that every person who has had to "come out" about something in their life has had unique experiences for which there is very little common thread. For sure, we can compare and contrast our stories, or how supportive loved ones are, or how we felt when talking about our secret for the first time; and we all might identify with certain parts of other's experiences, but they are all distinctly separate.

There is only one thing that everyone who has ever come out has experienced:

We did it.

One way or another, through hysterical laughter or baited breath, through erratic breathing or trickling tears, through awkward conversations or heartfelt letters, we tentatively opened a closet door and "came out."

And you can too.

In a perfect world, I don't think [one's sexual orientation] is anyone else's business, but I do think there is value in standing up and being counted.
– Anderson Cooper

I can't promise what your experience will be like. I can't promise it will be easy, or that you won't face hardships. I can't promise that everyone will accept you, or that you won't face heartbreak in light of rejection. What I can promise, however, is that you can do it. I don't know you, but I know you can do it. I don't know your background, or life, or your story, but you can do it. I believe in you.

That doesn't mean you are ready right now. Two years ago I toyed with the idea of coming out on October 11th, but I hadn't fully come out to myself yet. It would be months later before I would meekly mumble the words "I am bisexual" to my best friend from underneath a nest of fleece blankets. You might not be ready, and that's okay. Take your time, you deserve it.

I was certain that my world would fall apart if anyone knew. And yet when I acknowledged my sexuality I felt whole for the first time.
– Jason Collins

One by one, as if I were scheduling appointments for job interviews, I crept out of the closet to each of my friends. My identity shifted from bisexuality to homosexuality. I had a relatively privileged coming out experience, and know that I suffered much less rejection and pain than others did. Most of my pain was self-inflicted, a by-product of years of internalized self-hate.

We will all have different stories, but we all have stories worth telling. We all have lives worth living. And lives are not fully lived unless they are experienced authentically. You owe that to yourself. We *all* owe that to ourselves. Maybe that's what we all have in common too.

36

Read This If You're A High School Girl, And You Kind Of Hate Life Right Now

Marisa Donnelly

The world sees you, you know. On days when you don't feel beautiful. On mornings when you spend an hour in front of the bathroom mirror. You might think that your efforts are lost, that you're just a face in a sea of faces, but you're not. I promise you.

The world is too harsh, but also too quiet. You will hear the angry words the loudest. You will always see the stares rather than the smiles. I don't know why things are this way, and I'm sorry they are. But just know that you are seen. You are noticed.

Listen to me. You don't have to spend your mornings wondering if you are pretty, pressing your nose to the mirror and examining your pores and the bags under your eyes. We all have bags under our eyes. And wrinkles. And pimples. And freckles. And scars. And these are all the things that make us beautiful, make us unique.

I know you won't believe me now, but I'll tell you anyways. You don't need approval. You will never need approval. Your hair will always be too frizzy, or too straight, or too short, or too choppy. Your eyes will always be too round, or too blue, or too close together. Your body will always be too thick, or too fat, or too muscular, or too wide, or too tall, or too short, or too skinny. And even when you think you've become perfect, the world will turn away from you.

You'll be too perfect. And that won't be good enough either.

See, sweet girl, there's no winning. But that's okay.

Don't turn your face from the world. The world is not a negative place, just misunderstood. The world wants us to keep pushing, but you will see opposition to anything you do. This doesn't mean you should give up, this means you should fight back harder, be stronger.

You are more than a face in the mirror, you know. You are more than a body walking the halls of a high school, more than the catty girls and more than the eyeing boys. I know it seems like the most important thing is to be liked and loved, to fit in and to be recognized. But do not compromise yourself, do not change yourself, because you will spend years trying to rediscover that person you once were.

You are special, sweet girl. Special because you are young. Because you have your whole life to make mistakes, to fall in love, to meet your best friends, to hike mountains, to scuba dive, to learn how to cook, to kick box, to dream, to fall down and get back up again.

You will grow out of your pimples. You will grow into your long legs. You will learn that approval from friends and boys and the halls of high school doesn't compare to feeling good about yourself. Because life won't be easy, and your success will depend on your own strength, and your ability to pull yourself up from the ground.

I believe in you. I believe in what lies behind your face, your eyes. Behind that reflection in the mirror. It won't be easy right now, but you need to learn to believe in yourself.

Please, sweet girl, know that it will get better. The words you hear thrown around the halls, the hate and gossip that spills and seeps into your soul like spilled oil, will dissipate. You will look back one day and laugh at the girl who treated you so poorly because she taught you how to stand up for yourself. You will laugh at the boy who didn't give you the time of day, because he wants you now. You will laugh at the words of your friends, of your parents, of those who didn't understand. You will see it clearly—it all led you to where you are right now.

It will get better. The pain, the confusion, the way the world feels like it's crushing you from all sides as you plan for this unknown future that seems like an upside-down, directionless map. It will get better.

As you lean against your bathroom mirror, eyes squinted in disgust, know that you will never be good enough. You will always be nit-picked, always be judged, always be evaluated. But it's okay to never be good enough for the world. You won't. None of us will.

What matters is that you are good enough for yourself.

So stop worrying about the world and if the world will accept you. Accept yourself and smile at the mirror. And know that all the women who have survived high school are standing beside you in spirit, smiling at all our reflections.

37

Read This If You're Not Going To Be Home For The Holidays

Kovie Biakolo

What is your favourite Christmas song? According to a billboard chart dedicated exclusively to Christmas music, Mariah Carey's "All I Want for Christmas is You" is the most popular song in the United States. While Carey is a singer I feel privileged to have grown up listening to as I developed my own tastes in music, when I think of Christmas music, I don't think of "All I Want is You."

In the home I grew up in as in many other homes I'm sure, Christmas time meant Louis Armstrong's "Christmas in New Orleans," and Eartha Kitt's "Santa Baby," and of course that Nat King Cole favourite, "The Christmas Song," which is the fourth most popular Christmas track in the United States. As devout Catholics, Christmas was also about the many choruses and choral renditions of "Silent Night" and "Joy To The World" and "God Rest Ye Merry Gentlemen." For me, these songs make up the sounds of Christmas.

I still listen to most of these songs in my adulthood which bring back joyful memories — really, peaceful memories

— that I have of this time of year. In a way, they've become a saving grace to the other memories of Christmas somewhere between childhood and teenage years and adulthood that brought stress and sadness. Why do memories tend to work like that? Why does sadness sometimes seem to overwhelm joy?

Sadness, as you may or may not know, is another theme of the holiday season. It seems counterintuitive that a holiday that should be about the best things in life — music, food, family, friends, and goodwill — can in reality also become a time of year characterized by loneliness, disappointment, and anxiety. Indeed, it goes beyond sadness, and into a spike in medical depression.

Some of the reasons given for this sadness and even depression are: failed expectations, the stress of comparing your lives and livelihoods to family and friends, the propensity for this time of year to be for reflection — both good and bad, and as a co-worker put it, conducting "the annual happiness check." The annual happiness check, we determined, constitutes of mostly mandatory questions we ask when we gather with people periodically: "How's life?" "How's your job?" "Seeing anyone?" "Getting married soon?" "How are the kids?" All of which we have a tendency to respond superficially to, because who really wants to talk about the disappointments of their life in *the most wonderful time of the year*?

There is of course another reason that is more than just individual states of mind for which may bring the holiday blues. There is the reality of many who spend the holidays away from home. Home, of course, is not just a physical place, it is that invisible space where we feel love and safety in the midst of people who we care for, and who care for us, deeply, and if we're lucky, unconditionally.

But the disconcerting reality of life is not everyone can go home or has a home. There are those who may face financial restraints, and there are those who feel unwelcome by those who fate decided ought to be the people who should care for them, but don't. Yet still there are those who through dumb luck, difficult choices, lack of community, experience, and whatever else, do not have that physical homestead or that invisible but irreplaceable experience of *home*.

One of those is easier to cure than the other. In my adulthood, I have not always been able to make it to my homestead, to the physical (and sometimes changing) place where my parents and siblings and other family and friends may gather during this time of year. But I have mostly also found my home in those sweet family we choose, whom we call friends. I have said this many times in my twenties so far as a woman who has been far from family and often single: your friends are your family during this time of your life. It's why I put so much effort into my friendships – they have been my saving grace, my family, and my home.

But even still, a few Christmases ago, I found myself feeling that other lack of home. Far away, and in a particularly difficult year, and my stubborn refusal to reach out and "burden" my many homes that one year. I remember being at Christmas mass fighting back tears. The one place I will always feel safe enough to cry is church, but these were not the usual tears of relief or release, these were tears of loneliness. And I would eventually be rescued by unexpected friends that Christmas, because it is good to be with people. But I will never forget that feeling, and I will never wish it for anyone who knows me and considers me their home.

What I learned from that Christmas however, was one of the most important lessons I have had to learn. I learned that as much as we make homes with the families some of us are born into, and some of the good friends we consider family, we must also make a home in our own hearts; we must make a home in our *selves*. It's a lesson I think, that can only be learned through a lonely experience, but it was a lesson worth learning.

The other lesson I learned from that Christmas was opening your heart and home to some unexpected people. Interestingly, it's a lesson I learned in childhood too. See, every Christmas my mother would make us gather all the items we were no longer using and give them away to the less fortunate. And for much of my childhood, especially because my parents anniversary comes two days after Christmas, we would host friends and friends of friends at our home. So for me, the best of Christmas was about giving, sharing, and *being*.

In my lonely Christmas I was "rescued" by a friend and her friend — who probably didn't know they were rescuing me at the time. In truth, we were probably rescuing each other. But I would also spend some time with some of Chicago's homeless, who more than anything else, just want some company. I had spent many times working with the homeless in some shape or form, but never like this — never getting to know some of their most intimate stories. They were lonely and I was lonely, and although I had more to offer them in terms of the material things of life, in terms of what we had to offer each other beyond that, we were equals. We offered each other what we could: friendship, kindness, and loneliness.

I've decided I never again want to be as lonely as I was that Christmas. Which is probably why I'm writing this for those who think they might be, or who already are. To you, I say, tell people you want to be with them this time of year. Don't be stubborn. You are not a burden and you might be saving someone as much as they might be saving you. Open your homes and your hearts to unexpected friends and lonely strangers. Together, find that other home — that invisible space — where you can care for people deeply and maybe even unconditionally.

Most importantly, even through tears, put on some sounds of the Christmases that you've loved or the Christmases that you want to love, be the love you need, and make a home in your heart. After all, home needn't be in the past or somewhere in the future, home can be right now.

38

Read This If You're The Eternally Single Friend

Johanna Mort

"10 Things People Who Don't Really Have Any Exes Understand"

I've been sitting on this headline for three weeks now. It's relatable. It hasn't really been done before. It has the potential to be really funny.

But it's a lie.

It's my way of reaching out to the "Eternally Single" audience without actually admitting *how* eternally single I am. Later, I can write fun pieces about casual relationships or dating, and no one will think anything of it.

But the thing is, it's not that I don't *really* have any exes; I just don't have *any*. There aren't any shades of grey to the matter. I've never been on a date, and the number of people I've flirted with is very safely in the low single digits.

I haven't gone on a date with anyone partially because no one's ever asked, and partially because the idea of dating someone with a "normal" dating history is terrifying when I'm a 22-year-old with as many romantic experiences as my 10-year-old niece. I feel like I need to walk into any Tinder match with a giant asterisk:

BEWARE. THIS ONE HAS NO IDEA WHAT SHE'S DOING. APPROACH WITH CAUTION.

So each time I sat down to write my "fun, lighthearted" article, it always started out the same, with me extolling the virtues of being blissfully single:

> **1.** You get to occupy every corner of the bed!

> **2.** The only people that will break your heart are George RR Martin, Shonda Rhimes, and a particularly good Bon Iver track.

> **3.** You never have to worry about drunk-texting an ex! LOLOL life's great.

But soon enough, I start spiraling down into the rabbit-hole of singleness. The article doesn't feel honest unless it includes the not-so-great things about residing in Singletown, Population: 1.

> **4.** Friends who've dated or been in relationships will never TRULY understand what it feels like to be a romantic leper.

> **5.** No one takes your relationship advice seriously.

> **6.** You'll lie awake at night wondering what's so

wrong with you that romance in any form seems
to disapparate as soon as you enter the room.

It's right around this point that I always abandon the article, because it was forcing me to analyze a part of myself that I avoid at all costs.

I like to read books and watch *Doctor Who* and pretty much ignore any personal soliloquies that my brain runs on repeat like a *Law and Order: SVU* episode starring a now-famous actor.

Nothing good comes from wondering *why* I'm single and always have been, but that seems to be the only thing anyone wonders when they hear that the closest I ever got to a relationship was in sixth grade when a fellow 11-year-old *LIKE-liked* me for a month.

What? But you're such a nice girl! Any guy would be lucky to date you. Someone will come. Don't worry, you're just a late bloomer. There's nothing wrong with that.

Fuck late bloomers. I'm not a "late bloomer" because it implies that there's something wrong. That I fucked up and didn't fall into the same schedule as everyone else, and I'm the one running behind. That I haven't yet "bloomed," and only once other people start noticing how great I am will I finally "blossom" into the person I am supposed to be.

So here's my article:

3 Things People Who've Never Been In A Relationship Need To Know

1. There's nothing inherently wrong with you.

2. Your lack of a dating history doesn't define you.

3. Just because everyone else is doing things one way, doesn't mean you need to follow suit. Life isn't a straight line, and no one's path is going to look the same. Blaze your own trail.

This article isn't meant to be some feminist anthem or "Woe is Me" prose. It's just me finally being honest:

I'm single. I'm happy sometimes and I'm lonely other times. I don't think that makes me any different from anyone else.

Thought Catalog, it's a website.

www.thoughtcatalog.com

Social

facebook.com/thoughtcatalog
twitter.com/thoughtcatalog
tumblr.com/thoughtcatalog
instagram.com/thoughtcatalog

Corporate

www.thought.is

CPSIA information can be obtained
at www.ICGtesting.com
Printed in the USA
LVOW03s0017121117
555917LV00001B/3/P